S0-AUO-725

An
Autobiography
of a Person
in the Spirit

WITNESS LEE

Living Stream Ministry
Anaheim, California

© 1986 Living Stream Ministry

All rights reserved. No part of this work may be reproduced or transmitted in any form or by any means—graphic, electronic, or mechanical, including photocopying, recording, or information storage and retrieval systems—without written permission from the publisher.

First Edition, November 1986.

ISBN 0-87083-260-3 (hardcover)
ISBN 0-87083-261-1 (softcover)

Published by

Living Stream Ministry
2431 W. La Palma Ave., Anaheim, CA 92801 U.S.A.
P. O. Box 2121, Anaheim, CA 92814 U.S.A.

Printed in the United States of America
02 03 04 05 06 / 10 9 8 7 6 5 4

CONTENTS

FOREWORD

The chapters contained in this book are messages on 2 Corinthians that were given by Brother Lee in the summer of 1967 in Los Angeles, California. He states that the central thought of the Scriptures is that God intends to work Himself in Christ through the Spirit into us, that God and we, we and God, might be really one in life, in nature, and in the Spirit. Second Corinthians is the deepest book in the Bible to experientially unveil this intention. It is a book which is mostly on the subjective enjoyment and experience of Christ rather than doctrine.

Brother Lee also points out that 2 Corinthians may be considered as an autobiography of the Apostle Paul. If anyone is going to know what kind of a person Paul was, he must come to this book. In it we see a portrait of a person who lived in the spirit. For us to enjoy and experience Christ in a rich way we must be persons in the spirit as symbolized by ten aspects in 2 Corinthians—captives, letters, mirrors, vessels, ambassadors, co-workers, a temple, a virgin, lovers of the church, and tasters of Christ. It is by all these aspects that we can be thoroughly wrought by God and with God and be constituted the ministers of the new covenant for the building up of the church. It is our hope that the reader would pray much to be brought into the subjective reality of the riches of Christ as revealed in 2 Corinthians.

October, 1986   Benson Phillips
Irving, Texas

CHAPTER ONE

MINISTRY THROUGH THE CROSS

Scripture Reading: 2 Cor. 1:4-6, 8-9, 12, 19-22

In 2 Corinthians, Paul shows us that if we are going to have a ministry of Christ, we have to experience Christ by the working of the cross (1:9; 4:10-12), and the working of the cross is for us to experience the anointing, the sealing, and the pledge of the Holy Spirit (1:21-22). The ministry comes out of this experience. Second Corinthians gives us a pattern, an example, of how the killing of the cross works, how Christ is wrought into our being, and how we become the expression of Christ. These constitute the ministers of Christ and produce the ministry for God's new covenant. While Ephesians and Colossians may be the highest books in the Bible, 2 Corinthians is probably the deepest.

THE GOOD LAND, THE TEMPLE, AND THE BRIDE

The central thought of the Scriptures is that God intends to work Himself in Christ through the Spirit into us, that God and we, we and God, might be really one in life, in nature, and in the Spirit. To show this, God uses several figures or symbols in the Bible. First, He uses the figure of the good land (Exo. 3:8; Col. 1:12; 2:6-7). God saved and delivered Israel out of Egypt and brought them through the wilderness into the land of Canaan, which was the very enjoyment to the children of Israel (Deut. 8:7-10). The good land is a type of Christ for our enjoyment. God has delivered us out of the world, has brought us into Christ (1 Cor. 1:30), and has made Christ the good land to us that we may enjoy Him all the time. Whatever He is will be wrought into us (Gal. 1:16; 2:20;

4:19), and all His riches (Eph. 3:8) will be our enjoyment (Rom. 10:12). Then, in experience, we will be one with Christ.

Another major symbol in the Bible is the tabernacle or temple (John 1:14; 2:19-21; 1 Cor. 3:16-17; Eph. 2:21-22; Rev. 21:3, 22). In both the tabernacle and the temple there are the outer court, the holy place, and the Holy of Holies. If you are a priest of God up to the standard of His desire, you will be one in the Holy of Holies. To enjoy God by being mingled with Him is to be one with God in the Holy of Holies. To enjoy God in the Holy of Holies, in spirit (John 4:24), is to be mingled with Him (1 Cor. 6:17) as one in life and in nature (1 John 5:12; 2 Pet. 1:4).

Besides the good land of Canaan and the tabernacle or temple, there is another figure in the Bible concerning our enjoyment of Christ. This is the figure of the bride (John 3:29), the wife (Rev. 19:7), the virgin (2 Cor. 11:2). All the redeemed people of Christ are a bride, a virgin to Christ. We all have to be a bride and a virgin to Christ experientially that we may enjoy Him and that He may enjoy us, that we may be one with Him. Thus, in the Bible are these three types—the good land, the temple, and the bride, the wife, the virgin to Christ. These types may also be found, in particular, in 2 Corinthians.

In 1 Corinthians the believers were still in the wilderness, but not in the land of Canaan. They were still either in the flesh (the outer court) or in the soul (the holy place), but they were not yet in the spirit (the Holy of Holies). In 1 Corinthians 5:7 the Passover is mentioned. The people enjoyed the passover in Egypt. Then in chapter ten there are the manna and the living water out of the cleft rock (vv. 3-4). These items were also enjoyed by the people in the wilderness. In 1 Corinthians we cannot see anything of the children of Israel's entering into and enjoying the good land. Thus, the Apostle Paul encouraged them to press on (1 Cor. 9:24). The Corinthians may have had the spiritual gifts and knowledge, yet Paul told them that they were still fleshly (1 Cor. 3:1, 3) and soulish (2:14). They were not spiritual (3:1) because they were still acting and walking in the soul and flesh. Paul was encouraging them to press on to get themselves out of the realm of the soulish life that they might live in their spirit under the leading of the Spirit to enjoy Christ as their good land.

In 2 Corinthians Paul went on to tell them that he feared that they were distracted from Christ. They had been betrothed to Christ, but they were aiming at something other than Christ (11:2-3). Paul exhorted them to forget all the other aims to take Christ as their only aim. He is the Bridegroom and they were the bride. Second Corinthians shows us some persons who have really gotten into the good land and have enjoyed its riches. They have experienced Christ in the spirit to become part of the bride to Christ.

The experiences mentioned in this book are experiences in the Holy of Holies. This book gives a portrait of a person who is in the Holy of Holies. Paul and his co-workers were such persons. They had entered into the good land and were living in the spirit, experiencing Christ all the time. They were deep, even the deepest, in the experience of Christ.

It is rather hard for one to get any doctrine from this book. If one is trying to get doctrines out of this book, he is getting into the wrong field. In this field there are hardly any doctrines, but mostly experiences. These experiences are not in Egypt nor even in the wilderness but in the good land of Canaan. The experiences are not in the flesh nor in the soul but in the spirit. Paul did not exercise his fleshly wisdom but the spiritual wisdom which is God Himself. The experiences in this book are the deepest; they are experiences in the spirit, in the Holy of Holies. Brother Watchman Nee once told us that 2 Corinthians may be considered as the autobiography of the Apostle Paul. If you are going to know what kind of person the Apostle Paul was, you have to look into 2 Corinthians.

THE MINISTRY

Second Corinthians speaks concerning the ministry, which is constituted with, and produced and formed by, the experiences of the riches of Christ through sufferings, consuming pressures, and the killing work of the cross. The ministry is not merely a matter of gift. A person may be able to speak fluently and eloquently and give many good illustrations and proverbs, but this is just a gift. What the church, the Body, needs today is the ministry. The Body needs some brothers and sisters who have been thoroughly wrought by God and with God that they may have something of Christ, not merely in their mentality as knowledge to teach others, but as the very riches of Christ in their spirit and in their entire inward being to pass on to others. I expect that these ones will go out to certain places to have contact and fellowship with people. Eventually, you will see the growth in life and the building of the saints in the places that these ones visit. Today there are many teachings, much knowledge, and many gifts, but there is a great shortage of the ministry. We all have to be desirous of this kind of ministry. We need to pray, "Lord, be gracious to me that I might be delivered out of my concept concerning the gifts. How I long to be wrought through with something of God in Christ in the Spirit. May I have something of the divine element wrought into me to minister to others that I may have a divine ministry of Christ." The church needs the ministry much more than the gifts.

ENCOURAGED BY GOD

Second Corinthians 1:4-6 says, "Who encourages us in all our affliction, that we may be able to encourage those who are in every affliction through the encouragement with which we ourselves are encouraged by God. Because even as the sufferings of the Christ abound unto us, so through the Christ our encouragement also abounds. But whether we are afflicted, it is for your encouragement and salvation; or whether we are encouraged, it is for your encouragement, which operates in the endurance of the same sufferings which we also suffer." Pray-reading these verses again and again will help us to see that what the church needs today is the ministry. God encourages us in all our tribulations for a purpose—that we may be able to encourage others. The Greek word for encouragement in verse 4 also means comfort and consolation. To be encouraged by God means to be comforted and consoled by God.

THE WORKING OF THE CROSS

The more that the sufferings of Christ abound unto us, the more encouragement or refreshment we will be able to enjoy. If we are going to minister something of God in Christ to others, we have to suffer to have the experience. It is by the way of the cross that we may have some riches of Christ to minister to others. The ministry comes out in no other way but by the working of the cross.

Paul told us that God put him into a situation where he was "pressed out of measure" (1:8—KJV) or "excessively burdened" in order that he might be able to comfort others. You may have asked yourself why you have so many troubles. You may have trouble with your spouse, with your children, and even trouble with your physical body. Have you noticed that in this book there is the phrase "excessively burdened" or "pressed out of measure"? You may be pressed, but are you pressed out of measure? This means the working of the cross has terminated you, has brought you to an end.

Paul told us that he and his co-workers were excessively burdened beyond their power or strength so that they "despaired even of living" (1:8). Many of the young brothers have the strength. But sooner or later the Lord will press you again and again, and you will be trying to endure the suffering. Eventually you will say, "Lord, I give up my enduring because Your pressure is something far beyond my strength." When you are under a certain kind of suffering, never try to exercise your own strength to endure it by yourself. Never try to overcome it by yourself. You have to realize that eventually the Lord will press you beyond your strength. When the pressure comes, you may exercise all your strength—physically, mentally, and spiritually. But the more you exercise your strength, the more you will be pressed. Eventually, you will concede that the pressure is far beyond your strength. Praise the Lord for the pressing out of measure beyond our power!

After Paul told us that he and his co-workers were so burdened that they despaired even of living, he said, "But we ourselves had the sentence of death in ourselves, that we should not have confidence in ourselves, but in God, who raises the dead" (1:9). When the apostles were under the pressure of affliction, despairing even of life, they might have asked themselves what the issue of their suffering would be. The answer or response was death. The experience of death, however, ushers us into the experience of resurrection. Resurrection is the very God who resurrects the dead (John 11:25). The working of the cross terminates our self that we may experience God in resurrection. The experience of the cross always issues in the enjoyment of the God of resurrection. Such experience produces and forms the ministry (2 Cor. 1:4-6). This experience is further described in 4:7-12.

Paul's word shows us that we need to be terminated. We need to be brought to an end. Then we will learn not to trust in ourselves, but in God. For us to say that we need to trust in God and not in ourselves is easy, but to be wrought through in this matter needs a certain amount of experience. God is working through the cross to terminate us. God is working to bring us to an end, even to bring our spirituality, our spiritual attainment, to an end. You may trust so much in your spiritual attainment but even that has to be terminated.

In 1:12 Paul said, "For our boasting is this, the testimony of our conscience, that in singleness and sincerity of God, not in fleshly wisdom, but in the grace of God, we conducted ourselves in the world, and more abundantly toward you." In his conscience Paul had the testimony that he was walking, moving, having his being, on this earth not in fleshly wisdom but in the grace of God. To some, wisdom may be a clever way to meet a situation, but this wisdom comes from our flesh. Fleshly wisdom is what you yourself have in order to do something for yourself. The grace of God is that you do not do anything, but that God does everything within you. It is not that you do something to meet the situation, but that you let God do everything in you and for you. This is the grace of God.

Paul said that he conducted himself in the singleness and sincerity of God. Singleness can also mean simplicity. God is simple and God is single. The more that we are in the flesh and in the soul, the more complex we are. Then we do not have the simplicity but the complexity. A soulish person is very complex. But the more we are in the Holy of Holies, the spirit, the simpler we become. The more that we are in the spirit, the more we are simple and single. We are single in motive, single in aim, and single in all our desires. In 1:12 are the simplicity or singleness of God, the grace of God, and the sincerity of God. If we have been dealt with by the cross so that the cross has brought us to an end, we will be peaceful persons who are enjoying and experiencing the grace of God taking care of everything for us. We will be so simple and so single in our motive, in our aim. We will enjoy the grace of God and have the simplicity and the singleness of God.

THE ANOINTING, THE SEALING, AND THE PLEDGE OF THE SPIRIT

When the cross has been working through you, this working brings in resurrection. Therefore, 1:21-22 says that God has anointed us, has sealed us, and has given us the pledge, the foretaste, of the Spirit. If we are going to minister something of Christ to others, we have to experience Christ by the working of the cross, and the working of the cross is for the anointing, the sealing, and the pledge of the Spirit. The ministry comes out of this experience. We are now in Christ and Christ is our portion, but we experience Christ by the working of the cross. We need the working of the cross because we have the anointing, the sealing, and the foretaste, the earnest, of the Spirit within us. If you have not been brought to an end, it will be very difficult for you to take care of the inner anointing and the inner sealing. It will be hard for you to enjoy the inner pledge of the Spirit. The working of the cross is for the experience of the inner anointing, the sealing, and the inner enjoyment of the pledge of the Spirit. We all need the working of the cross that we may enjoy the pledge of the Spirit and that we may experience the anointing and the sealing of the Spirit.

The anointing is first, the sealing is second, and the pledge is third. God has anointed us with Himself. Anointing is like painting. The more a painter paints, the more the paint gets onto the thing that he is painting. Today God is the divine painter. He paints us with all the elements of Himself. The more He paints us with His divine elements, the more these elements of God will be wrought into us. Thus, God's anointing us is His imparting of all His divine elements into us. When we were unbelievers, we did not have the divine elements. We only had the human element. Since we have become believers, God is anointing Himself into us that we may have the divine elements dispensed into all our inward parts. God's anointing of Himself into us is so that we may be absolutely mingled with Him, with His divine elements, to be fully one with Him.

The anointing imparts God's elements into us and the sealing forms the divine elements into an impression to express God's image. If I take a seal and seal a piece of paper with it, the same figure of the seal is left on the paper. The sealing gives us the figure or the image. God has not only anointed us with all of His elements, but He has also sealed us with His own image. The more that we are sealed by God, the more we will have the image of God.

Finally, we have the pledge of the Spirit. The pledge of the Spirit is the foretaste of God as a sample and guarantee of the full taste of God. God has put Himself into us as a kind of down payment or foretaste so we can taste God within.

We must be impressed that God has anointed us with all His elements, has sealed us with His own image, and has put Himself into us as a kind of down payment for our enjoyment. We must learn how to realize the inner anointing, how to cooperate with the inner sealing, and how to enjoy the inner pledge, down payment, earnest, foretaste, of the Holy Spirit. We do this by the working of the cross. The cross has to bring us to an end. Then we can say, "Lord, now I have the sentence of death. I am despairing of my life. I am through. I am finished." Immediately we will sense the inner anointing, the inner sealing, and even the inner pledge of the Spirit. Through these three experiences of the anointing Spirit as the anointing, the sealing, and the pledge, with the experience of the cross, the ministry of Christ is produced. By the working of the cross with the inner anointing, sealing, and foretaste or pledge, we will have the adequate experience of Christ. Then we will have the ministry which the Body desperately needs today. May the Lord be merciful to us that we might be brought into the realization of how much we need the working of the cross to bring us to an end and of how much we need to experience the inner anointing, sealing, and pledge of the Spirit that we may have a real ministry for the Body of Christ.

CHAPTER TWO

A PERSON IN THE SPIRIT

Scripture Reading: 2 Cor. 1:9, 12; 2:13; 4:13, 16; 12:18; 10:3-4; 3:14; 4:4

If you get into the spirit of Paul's Epistles to the Corinthians, you can see that at the time Paul wrote these two books he had the history of the children of Israel as a background. The whole history of the children of Israel is a complete type of the experiences of the New Testament Christians (1 Cor. 10:6a, 11). Many Christians are clear that the Passover (1 Cor. 5:7), the exodus from Egypt (1 Cor. 10:1-2), the wandering in the wilderness (Heb. 3:7-19), and the enjoyment of the heavenly manna and the water out of the cleft rock (1 Cor. 10:3-4) are all types of our Christian experience today. But most Christians are not so clear that the entering into the good land and the living, walking, working, and laboring in the good land are also a type of our Christian experience (Col. 2:6-7). Our need is to know more and more about the living, the walking, the working, the laboring, and also the fighting of the people of Israel in the good land.

When Paul wrote these two letters, he must have had the background of this history. In 1 Corinthians 5:7 he said that Christ was our Passover. Then in chapter ten he told us that today we are enjoying the heavenly manna and are drinking the living water out of the cleft rock (vv. 3-4). This means that in 1 Corinthians the people had been brought out of Egypt and were wandering in the wilderness. This was the real situation of the Corinthians, and in this respect, many of today's Christians are Corinthians. We should not think that we are better than the Corinthians. Some talk about the heavenly church in the book of Ephesians, but not many are heavenly themselves. One can talk about the good land, about Canaan, but he may still be in Egypt or in the wilderness. When you are in your spirit, you are in the heavenlies (Eph. 2:6) because the heavenlies cannot be separated from your spirit. The heavenlies are in the spirit, and the spirit is in the heavenlies (see note 16[1] in Heb. 4—Recovery Version). Whenever you are living in the spirit, you are uplifted and you are in the heavenlies. But do you think that today you are walking completely in the spirit?

The Corinthians talked a lot about spiritual things, but they did so in a fleshly and soulish way. The Apostle Paul told them in the first book that they were fleshly and not spiritual (3:1). And in chapter two of the first book he spoke of soulish men (v. 14). A spiritual man (2:15) is one who does not behave according to the flesh nor act according to the soulish life, but lives according to the spirit, that is, his spirit (Rom. 1:9) mingled with the Spirit of God (Rom. 8:16; 1 Cor. 6:17). Such a one is dominated, governed, directed, moved, and led by such a mingled spirit. Although the Corinthians spoke much about spiritual things, the Apostle Paul designated them as fleshly and soulish. They were talking about spiritual things in the soul and in the flesh. Some may talk about the heavenly things in Ephesians, but they do so as Corinthians—in the soul or in the flesh.

Paul's second Epistle to the Corinthians is much deeper than the first. It seems that not many have paid attention to this second book. In Romans there is justification by faith, and in Ephesians is the church as the Body of Christ. But what is the subject of 2 Corinthians? What is the impression that you get from this book? I must tell you that this book is absolutely in the spirit. Many Christians are living in their flesh or soul, not in their spirit. Many know something about the Holy Spirit, but too few know about their human spirit in which the Holy Spirit dwells. (See *Our Human Spirit* published by Living Stream Ministry.) After the flesh and the soul in 1 Corinthians, we come to the spirit in 2 Corinthians. After the outer court and the holy place, we come to the Holy of Holies; after Egypt and the wilderness, we come to the good land, the land of Canaan. In this book you can see the good land. You can also see the practical life in the Holy of Holies. In this book you can see some human beings absolutely in the spirit.

NOT TRUSTING IN OURSELVES, BUT IN GOD

In 2 Corinthians 1, Paul told us that he and his co-workers were "excessively burdened, beyond our power, so that we despaired even of living" (v. 8). They had the sentence of death in themselves that they should not trust in themselves but in the very God who raises the dead (v. 9). We need to be impressed with these words in 1:9—"we should not have confidence in ourselves, but in God." Through the redemption of Christ, the very God, who is in the heavens, has come into us, into our spirit (Col. 1:27; 2 Tim. 4:22). Thank the Lord that He is now in our spirit, calling us to forget about the soulish things and turn to our spirit to meet Him. We should no longer trust in our self, in our soul, but in God who is in our spirit.

We may know the doctrine concerning no longer trusting in ourselves but in God. To say that we trust in God is easy, but in our experience it may be different. If a husband's wife is not so nice to him, the first thing he usually does is to exercise his mind to consider his wife's situation. This is what it means to trust in yourself. If we have really learned the lesson to trust no more in ourselves, we would not exercise our mind first but our spirit. Immediately, we should turn to our spirit and exercise our spirit to contact God. This practically means that we do not trust in ourselves but in God. We all need this kind of experience today.

NOT IN FLESHLY WISDOM, BUT IN THE GRACE OF GOD

In 1:12 Paul said that he conducted himself "not in fleshly wisdom, but in the grace of God." To trust in the self is bad, but to have fleshly wisdom is worse. Paul did not say human wisdom but fleshly wisdom. We generally understand that wisdom has something to do with the mind, but Paul speaks of a kind of wisdom related to the flesh. Fleshly wisdom is versus the grace of God. Fleshly wisdom is something connecting the soul and the flesh. The grace of God is in the spirit, working through the soul and the body. We trust in God, and this God is working within us. Grace is the very God who is working within us. He is working from within our spirit through our soul and body in order that our whole being will be under His working. We should have no trust in ourselves but in God.

Our conversation, our walk, our living in this world should not be something in our fleshly wisdom but in the grace of God. This means that we have stopped all our doings and that it is now God who is working within us from our spirit through our soul and body. Our whole being is under the working of God. This kind of person is living and walking in the Holy of Holies all the time.

IN MY SPIRIT

Because Paul was such a person living in the Holy of Holies, he could say, "I had no relief in my spirit" (2:13). Paul did not say that he had no relief in his mind or in his heart. If you are going to understand 2 Corinthians you have to pick up the key phrases such as "not have confidence in ourselves, but in God"; "not in fleshly wisdom, but in the grace of God"; and "no relief in my spirit." Paul did not even say that he had no relief in the Spirit but "in my spirit." Paul was a person living, walking, working, and even having his being in his spirit. He was not a man living in the soul or the flesh but a person living in the spirit. Thus, he could say that he had no relief in his spirit.

This shows us that Paul did not care for the circumstances or for what he thought or could see. He only cared for his spirit. His brother Titus had not come, so he did not have the relief in his spirit. I like this term—"in my spirit." We have to be brought into the realization of our spirit, and we have to learn how to do everything in our spirit. If we are going to be happy, we have to be happy in the spirit. If we are going to be sorrowful, we have to be sorrowful in the spirit. Many times we are happy merely in our emotions. We may not know how to be happy in the spirit. But we have to learn how to be happy in the spirit, how to have the relief in our spirit. We all need to learn to take care of the relief in our spirit, and be persons living in the spirit.

Then in 4:13 Paul tells us that he and the brothers with him had "the same spirit of faith." We all have to learn to exercise the spirit to such an extent. Whatever we do, whatever we say, we have to be sure that we have the same spirit, that we are in the same spirit. This is not something in the soul or in the flesh but in the spirit. When we go to see a brother, we have to go in the spirit. When we have fellowship, we must have it in the spirit.

THE OUTWARD MAN DECAYING, YET THE INWARD MAN BEING RENEWED

Verse 16 of chapter four says, "Wherefore we do not lose heart, but if indeed our outward man is decaying, yet our inward man is being renewed day by day." The inward man is our regenerated spirit as the life and person with our renewed soul as its organ. The outward man is our body as the organ with our soul as its life and person. The outward man is perishing, decaying, or being weakened, reduced, and consumed. But the inward man is being renewed, refreshed, encouraged, and strengthened by being nourished with the fresh supply of the resurrection life. As our mortal body, our outward man, is being consumed by the killing work of death, our inward man, that is, our regenerated spirit with the inward parts of our being (Jer. 31:33; Heb. 8:10; Rom. 7:22, 25), is being metabolically renewed day by day with the supply of the resurrection life.

The outward man has to be consumed. It is decaying and being reduced. The inward man has to be encouraged, refreshed. To understand the full meaning of what Paul says here, we have to put the first four chapters together. In the first chapter he told us that he was pressed out of measure (v. 8). Then in the fourth chapter he showed us how he was pressed on every side or afflicted in every way (v. 8). Verses 7 through 18 of chapter four show that the apostles lived a crucified life in resurrection, or the resurrection life under the killing of the cross, for the carrying out of their ministry. Paul was much afflicted and perplexed, but he realized that these afflictions and perplexities were doing a good job to reduce the outward man. But while the outward man was being reduced, the inward man was being refreshed and encouraged day by day. This means that we have to be kept away from our soul, the wilderness, the Holy Place. We must be kept fully and solely in the Holy of Holies. We have to live and act in the Holy of Holies.

To argue with people is to nourish or feed your soulish life. The more you argue, the stronger the outward man is. Sometimes a wife and a husband are tempted to quarrel or debate. Suppose that the wife is angry, but the brother would not say a word to his wife to argue with her. The brother may say that he did not say a word because he has learned to suffer. This way of acting, however, is not the Christian way, but it may be the way of the followers of Confucius or Buddha. If you would ask me why I do not argue with my wife, I would say that I do not like to feed or to nourish my soul. The more I argue with my wife, the more I feed my soul. We have to learn the lesson to starve the soul, to reduce the soul. The outward man should be reduced. We must realize that everything that happens to us has a purpose. God's purpose is for our outward man to be reduced so that the inward man can be strengthened, refreshed, encouraged, nourished, and renewed day by day.

When our outward man is reduced and our inward man is renewed, we are kept in the Holy of Holies. It is here in the Holy of Holies, in our spirit, that we enjoy and experience Christ. It is here that you experience all the divine things with God and in God. Gradually we ourselves will become a ministry. We will not merely be a minister but a minister with a ministry. Then we will minister life, God, and the riches of Christ to others. We will not just pass on certain teachings, doctrines, and knowledge to others. Whatever we do will be a ministering of Christ, of God, into others. This is the need today.

WALKING IN THE SAME SPIRIT

In 2 Corinthians 12:18 Paul said that he and Titus walked in the same spirit. This verse and the other verses we have fellowshipped show us what kind of person the Apostle Paul was. He was a person fully, absolutely, and thoroughly living in the spirit. He would never be kept away from the spirit.

CAPTURING THE THOUGHTS
UNTO THE OBEDIENCE OF CHRIST

Because Paul lived in the spirit, he learned the lesson of how to deal with people's thoughts. In 2 Corinthians there are three passages related to the matter of thoughts. In 3:14 Paul told us that the thoughts of the children of Israel were "hardened." Then in 4:4 he said that the thoughts of the unbelieving have been "blinded" by the god of this age. Finally, in 10:5 Paul indicated that the thoughts needed to be captured to obey Christ. The thoughts can be hardened by the self, blinded by the god of this age, or be captured by the ones who have the ministry. They are captured by those who war, who fight the battle, not according to the flesh but with the weapons which are powerful to God (v. 4). When you have the ministry, when you are a person really living, walking in the spirit, you are not fighting the battle according to the flesh, but you are equipped, qualified, to do a work to capture the thoughts of people, to bring all their thoughts into captivity to the obedience of Christ.

You can never subdue people by arguing. The more you argue, the more you stir up the thoughts of people. Some people may come to you to challenge you to argue with them, but if you argue with them, you will only stir up their thoughts. However, if you are a person who has the ministry within, you will be qualified and equipped with the spiritual weapons that are powerful to God to cast down or overthrow the reasonings and to take captive every thought unto the obedience of Christ.

WHAT THE CHURCH NEEDS TODAY—
THE MINISTRY OF CHRIST

In 1 Corinthians there are the gifts, the knowledge, and the teachings. But in 2 Corinthians we cannot find these things. Neither can we find miracles or healings. Instead we find a thorn in Paul's flesh that the Lord refused to remove even after Paul entreated Him three times (12:7-9).

Paul asked the Lord to perform a miracle by taking away the thorn, but the Lord refused to do it. In this book we do not see miracles but sufferings. In 2 Corinthians there are no miracles, no healings, and no gifts, but suffering to reduce the outward man that the ministry might be produced. The more we suffer and the more the outward man is reduced, the more we will have of the ministry. Then we will have something of the riches of Christ to minister to others. This is the need of the church today. The church is not in great need of miracles, gifts, teachings, or knowledge. Today the church needs the ministry of Christ. History has shown us that something may be built up by the gifts, but eventually what is built up will be torn down by the same gifts. This is a tragic story that has been repeated many times.

If we would be humbled by the grace of the Lord and learn how to live in the spirit, the sovereign Lord will assign each one of us a certain amount of suffering. The more we love the Lord Jesus, the more we will suffer something and the more we will be reduced. Eventually, a certain amount of ministry will be produced, and the church will be built up. This is what the church needs today.

CHAPTER THREE

CAPTURED BY CHRIST

Scripture Reading: 2 Cor. 2:14-16; 3:3-6

As we have seen in the past two chapters, 2 Corinthians gives us a full portrait of a person living in the presence of God, that is, in the Holy of Holies. After chapter one, the Apostle Paul starts to tell us what kind of person he is as he is living in the Holy of Holies. He mentions a number of aspects of such a person who is living in the presence of God, in the Holy of Holies, all the time.

CAPTIVES OF CHRIST

The first aspect of a person living in the Holy of Holies all the time can be seen in 2:14 where Paul says, "But thanks be to God, who always leads us in triumph in the Christ." W. J. Conybeare, in his translation of 2 Corinthians, tells us that the Greek word for "leads us in triumph" was a special word used in ancient times to describe a triumphal procession. In the Roman Empire, when a general won a battle, he captured many captives. Then in the capital there was a celebration of the victory, and in that celebration there was a triumphal procession with many captives to make a show of the victory gained by the general. The Apostle Paul adopted this expression to show that Christ is the General who gained the victory and that God today is celebrating Christ's victory.

Among so many who have been captured by Christ, Paul was one. He was one of the biggest opponents to Christ and to His gospel. One day on the road to Damascus, he was conquered, subdued, captured (Acts 9:1-9). From that day he became a captive of Christ. We may think that Paul was going out to travel here and there as a wonderful preacher. But according to his feeling, he was in the triumphal procession of Christ as a captive. God is celebrating the victory of Christ with a triumphal procession, with a train of captives. Paul was a captive in the celebration of Christ's victory. He had been captured by Christ.

The first aspect of a person living in the Holy of Holies is that of a captive. First of all, we have to be captives of Christ in the train, in the procession, of the celebration of Christ's victory. If we are going to live in the Holy of Holies, to enjoy Christ as the good land, to be in the spirit, we must first be captured by Christ. Christ has to conquer us, subdue us, and capture us. Truthfully speaking, many of us must admit that instead of us being captives to Christ, Christ is a captive to us. All day you are celebrating your victory, with Christ as a captive in the train of your celebration. In your experience who is the captive—Christ or you? Who is celebrating the victory? Who is defeated—you or Christ? Many of us have to admit that nearly all the time, Christ our Savior has been defeated and captured by us, becoming our captive in the train of the celebration of our fleshly victory.

This is the challenge in this chapter—a person living in the Holy of Holies must be a captive in the train of Christ's triumphal procession, celebrating Christ's victory on the cross. In so many things and nearly in all things we are not subdued or conquered by Christ. It may be that our will, the human will, the self-will, has never been conquered. On the one hand, you as a believer are a slave to Christ. But on the other hand, you are still an opponent, an enemy, to Christ because even until now your will has not been subdued or conquered. We should consider whether or not our desire has been conquered by Christ. I realize from my own experiences that even in seeking spiritual things we may still be an enemy of Christ. While we are seeking spiritual things, we are still an opponent to Christ because we seek spiritual things in our way according to ourselves, according to our desire. You may be seeking the Lord, yet be seeking Him according to your will. On the one hand, you are a seeker of the Lord, but on the other hand, you are an opponent to Christ. We all must realize that we first have to be conquered. We have to be defeated, praying from the depths of our being, "Lord, defeat me. Be merciful to me and never let me have the victory. O Lord, how dangerous and how pitiful it would be if You would allow me to have the victory. Lord, keep me defeated." Day by day there are many struggles, not between you and the world, but between you and the Lord. Day by day there are many battles, not between you and sins, but between you and the Lord. Do not focus on the world or sins, but take care of the battle between you and the Lord. If you would only be willing to be defeated by the Lord, all the world and all the sins would be under your feet. Why are you defeated by the world? Because you defeated Christ. Why are you defeated by any besetting sin? Because you are defeating Christ all the time. I hope that you would concentrate your prayer on this one thing—"Lord, make me Your captive. Never let me win. Defeat me all the time." After praying in this way, you will see what will happen to you. All the self will, self desire, self emotion, self thoughts, and so many things of the self are still existing with you, and day by day, hour after hour, Christ has been defeated by you. This is the problem.

We may think that we are called to serve the Lord, that we are going to do some work for the Lord. We may think that we are serving the Lord in an absolute way, but we do not know how many rebellious elements are within us. The germs, the elements of rebellion are still within us, so we have to be defeated, conquered, subdued, and eventually carried away as a captive in the triumphal procession of Christ's victory. Second Corinthians is not a book of doctrine but the autobiography of a person who considered himself as a captive in the train of the triumphal procession of God's celebration of Christ's victory over His enemies. Paul said that God "always leads us in triumph." When I was young, I thought this was my triumph. Today, though, I realize that this is not my triumph but His triumph. God always leads us as a captive in the triumph of Christ.

Are you willing to be a captive? You need to tell yourself and tell the Lord that you are willing to be a captive of Christ. If only a small number of people would be willing to be captives of Christ in His triumphal procession, the entire United

States would be greatly affected. Many seek for gifts of power, but what the church needs, what the world needs, is not a gifted person but a captured person. Today what the church needs is not a spiritual giant but a little captive. In this universe and on this earth, God is celebrating the triumph of His Son, Christ. Are you willing to be just a little captive in this celebration? If you are willing, then wherever you go something will happen. Person after person will be captured. Just as you are a captive, they also will become captives of Christ. We may consider the Apostle Paul as a great preacher, but he considered himself as a captive. God leads us as captives in the triumph of Christ, celebrating His victory. We all have to be willing to be Christ's captives.

I believe that a great number of young people today are ready and willing to serve the Lord, but I am greatly concerned that their seeking is along the lines of power, gifts, teachings, and knowledge. This seeking is on the wrong track. First, you have to be conquered, defeated, and captured by Christ. We all need to bow our knees and say to Him, "Lord, I am willing to be Your captive."

LETTERS OF CHRIST

After Paul tells us that he is a captive in chapter two, he goes on to tell us that we have to be letters of Christ in 3:3. The second aspect of a person who lives in the spirit, the Holy of Holies, is that he is a letter. In 3:3 Paul said that "you are a letter of Christ ministered by us, inscribed not with ink, but with the Spirit of the living God." A letter is something that has been written. But if you have never been captured by Christ, you could never be written on by the Spirit of the living God. First, we have to be captured. To be captured by Christ means that our emotions are subdued, our will is subdued, and even our desires are captured. Then the Spirit has a free way to write on us whatever He wants to write of Christ. Christ has been put into you (Col. 1:27), and as the Spirit (2 Cor. 3:17) He is within you to write the elements, the riches, of Christ into your whole being. But if you are rebellious in your mind, in your emotions, and in your will, there is no way for the Spirit of Christ to write something of Christ into your being. He is waiting for you to be willing to be captured by Christ. If you are conquered, defeated, subdued, and captured by Christ, you will be a good piece of paper for the Spirit's writing.

You may think that you are able to go out to do some work for the Lord, but you may merely be "a piece of blank paper" with not much of Christ written into you. How much of Christ can others read in your being? This is not merely a matter of speaking or preaching, but a matter of being read by others. How much of Christ can be seen or read by others in you? This depends upon how much of Christ has been written into you.

The inner working of the indwelling Christ is an inner writing. The Spirit of the living God is within you waiting all the time for a chance to write something of Christ into your being, into your inward parts. But I say again that until you are willing to be captured by Christ, the Holy Spirit can write nothing of Christ into you. Christ is in your spirit (2 Tim. 4:22), but He is not so much in your mind, emotion, and will. You have Christ within you, but you may be rebellious in your mind, emotion, and will. Now you need to be defeated, conquered, subdued, not doctrinally but practically in your mind, emotion, and will. When you are really subdued by Christ, the Holy Spirit, who is the Spirit of Christ within you, will have the chance, the free way, to write something of Christ gradually into every part of your being. Paul uses the word "inscribed," not merely written. Christ is inscribed into every part of our inner being with the Spirit of the living God to make us His living letters, that He may be expressed and read by others in us.

I am for the study of the Bible, but if you study the Bible only with the desire to get the knowledge of the letters, you will get very little. It is not the knowledge of the letters, but the Spirit that gives life (3:6); it is not the teachings, but the Spirit that gives life. If you consider that to read or to study the Word of God is merely to get some knowledge or teaching, you are absolutely wrong. To read and to study the Word is mainly to feed your inner man, to nourish your inner man, not merely to get the knowledge (Jer. 15:16; 1 Tim. 4:6).

Regardless of how much knowledge we get from the Bible, if we are not subdued by Christ and being written into with the Spirit of the living God, we can do nothing for the Lord in a way which will really build up His Body.

If we are going to build up His Body, first of all, we ourselves have to be defeated. We have to be conquered. Then we will be under the inner writing of the Spirit all the time. There will be a writing, an inscribing, of Christ going on within us, not by the letters of knowledge in our mind, but by the living Spirit in and out from our spirit. Some element of Christ will be inscribed, will be wrought, into the inward parts of our whole being. Something of Christ will be inscribed into our mind, our emotion, our will, and our whole person, our whole being, will become a letter of Christ. It is not merely that you go out to preach Christ by your speaking, but that you are a person with Christ inscribed into your being as a living letter of Christ. Wherever you go people can see and read something of Christ within you.

This is a matter of the ministry, not of gift. You may receive a gift in an instant, but if you are going to have a ministry, you will need an amount of time to be conquered, subdued, and captured by Christ. Eventually, the way will be paved for the indwelling Christ to write Himself gradually, little by little, into your being. Then you become a minister with a ministry, not merely a gifted person with a gift.

Whatever has been revealed in the Scriptures has to be written or inscribed into you, not merely by your studying of the Word or your reading of the Bible but by your being willing to be captured by Christ. Many Christians think that if they hear better messages to acquire more Bible knowledge, they will become better believers. This is a wrong understanding. To be a minister with a ministry to build up the Body of Christ is not a matter of receiving better teachings or a certain help from hearing messages, but a matter of Christ inscribing Himself into us in a living, real, active, and practical way.

How much we need to pray-read the verses in this chapter in a desperate way! You may even fast and pray, "Lord, in my whole life I have never been conquered by You. I have been seeking, but I have never been conquered or captured by You. I am so rebellious toward You in my mind, emotion, and will. Lord, I am fasting for this matter. Be merciful to me and conquer and capture me." You need such a specific prayer to the Lord. Then you will be a good piece of paper for the living Spirit to inscribe all the riches of Christ into your being. God will accomplish something through you as a captive and as a living letter of Christ.

CHAPTER FOUR

REDUCED TO THE SPIRIT

Scripture Reading: 2 Cor. 1:17-20; 2:10; 10:1; 11:10; 12:9;
13:14, 3-5

We have seen that the Apostle Paul shows us in 2 Corinthians how he was a person absolutely in the spirit. He was a person taught by God, tested by God, and even trained by God not to live in the flesh but in the spirit. In previous chapters, we began to see that what the church needs today is not a person full of knowledge, full of education, or full of gifts and power, but a person who is reduced in the natural, outward man (4:16). The outward man has to be consumed, reduced, all the time. Then we will be reduced into the spirit, and we will learn how to live absolutely in the spirit. This is the kind of person the church needs today. Throughout the history of the church, there have been many spiritual giants, gifted persons, and great teachers, but the church has not been built up. The Lord needs some people who have been reduced to the spirit for the building up of the church, His Body.

We must realize that the Lord is coming back soon. The Lord told us that He would come quickly (Rev. 22:20), but one may think His coming has been slow because it has been nearly two thousand years since His ascension. But do not forget that to Him one thousand years are as one day (2 Pet. 3:8). Through my study of prophecy, I was deeply impressed that the prophetic writings stressed the reformation of the nation of Israel (see Matt. 24:32 and notes). The nation of Israel was reformed in 1948, and Jerusalem was returned to Israel in 1967. This was the marvelous doing of the Lord. No one dreamed that the nation of Israel could be reformed or that Jerusalem could be returned to Israel in such a way.

The fulfillment of this prophecy shows us that the Lord is preparing Israel and the church for His coming back. The Lord has done something to fulfill His prophecy concerning Israel, and I do believe that the Lord will do something quickly to prepare His bride. We have seen that the Lord prepares His bride not merely by gifts or by teaching but by the working of the cross and the anointing of the Spirit. We have to be reduced, and we have to be conquered, captured, by Christ.

We all have to be reduced to the spirit. Our spirit is not empty, is not vacant, but it is occupied by Christ. Christ is in our spirit (2 Tim. 4:22). When we are reduced into the spirit, we meet Christ. Therefore, to be reduced to the spirit means to be reduced to Christ, to be reduced to live by Christ. Second Corinthians 3:17 is a vital and precious verse telling us that Christ the Lord is the Spirit. Christ today is the indwelling Spirit within our spirit. As the indwelling Spirit, He is now living, moving, acting, and even waiting for us to be reduced into the spirit. We have to be reduced into the spirit. Once we are reduced into the spirit, we meet Christ. Second Corinthians, on the one hand, shows us that the Apostle Paul was reduced to the spirit. On the other hand, it shows us how this apostle lives, acts, and works in the spirit by Christ.

THE PERSON OF CHRIST

Second Corinthians 2:10 mentions "the person of Christ." The American Standard Version translates this phrase as "the presence of Christ." In the original Greek text the common word for presence is *parousia.* But the word for person here is *prosopon.* Paul said, "But whom you forgive anything, I also forgive; for what I also have forgiven, if I have forgiven anything, it is for your sake in the person of Christ." Paul forgave a brother in the person of Christ. This Greek word means the face, the part around the eyes, which is the index of all the inward thoughts and feelings to signify the presentation of the whole person. The part of the face around the eyes is the index of all the inward thoughts and feelings, signifying what a person is thinking and how he feels within. Paul forgave that brother in the person of Christ, according to the index of His whole person expressed in His eyes. Paul lived not only in the presence of the Lord but also in the index of the inward feelings and thought of Christ. This is so deep, so tender, and so delicate.

Once I was invited to the home of a dear Christian couple. As I was there, I observed that the brother behaved himself not only in the presence of his wife but also in the person of his wife. Just by looking into her eyes, he could tell whether or not she approved of what he was doing. Not a word needed to be spoken. This particular husband had learned to move in the person of his wife.

I cannot fully express the feeling I had within when I discovered the meaning of this word "person." I bowed before the Lord and said, "Lord, for all these years I have never realized that I have to live not merely in Your presence but in Your person in such a tender way." It is not just to live in His presence, but even more in His person. I do not think that we Christians behave ourselves in the person of the Lord in such a tender way. We may say that we live, act, and behave in the presence of the Lord, but who behaves himself in the person of Christ, in the way that brother behaved himself in the person of his wife? But here in 2:10 there is a phrase telling us that Paul was such a person, behaving himself all the time in the index of the Lord's eyes, the index of His inward feelings and thoughts, in His person.

Paul looked at the index of the Lord's eyes, and he knew that he had to forgive that brother. He forgave him not according to his feeling, not according to his thought, but according to the feeling, the thought, of the Indweller within him. He was behaving himself in the person of Christ. When he forgave, he forgave in the person of Christ. He wanted to let the Corinthians know that he did not forgive according to himself or according to his flesh but in the person of Christ. This is what it means to live by Christ. The Apostle Paul had been reduced to such an extent that he never behaved himself in his person. He behaved himself in the person of Christ, in the face, in the thought, in the expression of the feeling and the thought of Christ. To live in the person of Christ is so tender and so deep.

Paul was a person reduced to nothing except taking Christ as his person. He behaved himself in the person of Christ.

THE CHANGELESSNESS OF CHRIST

In 2 Corinthians 1:17 Paul says, "This therefore intending, did I then use fickleness? Or the things which I resolve, do I resolve according to the flesh, that with me there should be yes, yes and no, no?" Paul did not purpose things according to the flesh so that he said yes at one time and no at another time. He was not a fickle person of yes and no. Paul was a person with whom there was no fickleness. When he said yes, he said it with Christ. When he made a decision, he made it with Christ. When Christ said yes, he said yes. When Christ said no, he said no. There was no fickleness, no changing with Paul because he said yes not by himself, not according to the flesh, but according to the indwelling Christ.

In 1:18-20 Paul says, "But God is faithful, that our word toward you is not yes and no; for the Son of God, Christ Jesus, who was preached among you through us, through me and Sylvanus and Timothy, did not become yes and no, but in Him is yes. For whatever promises of God there are, in Him is the Yes; wherefore also through Him is the Amen to God, for glory through us." With Christ there is no changing. Since the Christ whom Paul preached according to God's promises did not become yes and no, the word he preached concerning Him was not yes and no. Not only his preaching but also his living was according to what Christ is. He was not a man of yes and no, but a man who was the same as Christ. He was a person living by Christ. When he said yes, he said it with Christ. In himself Paul had been reduced to nothing, so he could say that the yes of Christ was his. Christ is not yes and no, but He is always the same. Paul was always the same because he lived by Christ.

We need to pray that the Spirit would help us to realize and to see what kind of person the Apostle Paul was when he was on this earth. He was a person absolutely reduced to nothing, but taking Christ as everything in his spirit. We all have to be reduced to such an extent that we are in our spirit taking Christ as everything. When we say yes to people, we should say it with Christ. If Christ would not say yes, we should not say yes. We have no position, right, or standing to say anything apart from Christ because we have been crucified with Him (Gal. 2:20). Paul had been reduced to the spirit. He had been pressed out of measure (2 Cor. 1:8) so that it was no longer him but Christ who lived in him. Even when he said yes, he said it with Christ.

We may love the Lord and try to live by Christ, but how many of us practice this whenever there is a question for us to answer? Do you consider answering it with Christ? This is why some of the brothers are always changing—in the morning it is "yes," but in the afternoon it is "no." They are changing all the time. But if you would take Christ as your answer, as your Yes, as your Amen, there would be no changing. Christ is always the same (Heb. 13:8) and the Apostle Paul took Christ as his yes.

THE MEEKNESS
AND FORBEARANCE OF CHRIST

In 10:1 Paul says, "But I myself, Paul, entreat you through the meekness and forbearance of Christ." We may be meek and forbearing but is our meekness and forbearance something of Christ? We all agree that we have to reject or repudiate the character that is not meek and forbearing. But have you ever realized that you have to reject your meekness and your forbearance? Some brothers and sisters may be proud of their meekness and forbearance. A certain sister may have an inward attitude that she is more meek than other sisters. But the Apostle Paul said that he entreated the Corinthians, not in his own meekness or forbearance but in the meekness and forbearance of Christ. This again shows us a person living in the spirit, always taking Christ as his everything. He experienced Christ not only as his power, but also as his meekness and forbearance. He was a person living by Christ.

THE TRUTH OF CHRIST

In 11:10 Paul says, "The truth of Christ is in me." We all would say that we have to reject the lies and speak the truth, but have you ever asked yourself whose truth you speak? Do you speak the truth of Christ or do you speak your own truth? Paul said that the truth of Christ was in him. We have to speak the truth of Christ, not the truth of the human nature, of the old man, of the self. We have to learn to not only repudiate all the lies but to also renounce or reject our truth. You have to repudiate your truth as well as your lies; then you could take the truth of Christ. Paul forgave in the person of Christ; he entreated in the meekness and forbearance of Christ; and he said the truth of Christ was in him. Since the apostle lived by Christ, whatever Christ was became his virtue in his behavior.

THE POWER OF CHRIST

In chapter thirteen Paul told us something concerning the power of Christ (vv. 3-5). The power of Christ is not experienced when we are powerful but when we are weak. Paul said, "Whenever I am weak, then I am powerful" (2 Cor. 12:10). It is harder to be weak than it is to be powerful. Paul said that Christ was "crucified out of weakness" (13:4). We realize that Christ was the almighty God, but at the time He was crucified, He became weak. If He had not become weak, how could human beings have crucified Him? As the almighty, all-powerful God, how could He have been arrested? Who could put Him on the cross? But He was willing to be weak, and He became weak. Therefore, the Apostle Paul said, "We are weak in Him" (v. 4).

Have you ever learned the lesson to be weak in Christ? We always like to talk about being powerful in Christ, but have we ever tried to be weak in Christ? The power of Christ could never be perfected or manifested until we are weak. The power of Christ, which is His grace to us, is perfected in our weakness (12:9). When we are weak, we may experience the power of Christ in our weakness. Again we see that 2 Corinthians shows us a person who has been reduced to nothing, with no strength, that the power of Christ might be perfected in his weakness. Here is a person absolutely reduced to nothing but taking Christ as everything.

THE GRACE OF CHRIST
AND CHRIST SPEAKING IN HIM

In 13:14 Paul refers to the grace of Christ and in 13:3 he says that Christ is speaking in him. Again we see a person that has been reduced to nothing but Christ. Christ speaks in him. Christ's person is his person; Christ's meekness is his meekness; Christ's forbearance is his forbearance; Christ's truth is his truth; Christ's power is his power; and Christ's grace is his grace. Whatever he is is Christ. This is a person who is living in the spirit.

CHAPTER FIVE

MIRROR, CAMERA, AND VESSEL

Scripture Reading: 2 Cor. 3:13-18; 4:3-11; 16-18

We have seen that a person who is living in the presence of the Lord, that is, in the spirit, in the Holy of Holies, is likened to a captive in a celebrating procession and to a letter. If we mean business with the Lord and desire to follow Him in the spirit, we have to be captives and we have to be inscribed with the Spirit of the living God to be the letters of Christ to express Him. In this chapter we want to see two more aspects of a person who is living in the Holy of Holies.

A MIRROR BEHOLDING AND REFLECTING THE GLORY OF THE LORD

Second Corinthians 3:18 tells us that we need to be mirrors beholding and reflecting the glory of the Lord. A mirror reflects whatever it beholds. When we are beholding the Lord, we reflect the Lord. However, if a veil is placed over the mirror, nothing is reflected. Paul tells us that we need to behold the Lord with an unveiled face. We need to ask what the veil is that Paul is talking about. Some may feel that the veil here is the flesh referred to in Hebrews 10:20. But the veil in Hebrews 10 is not the veil in 2 Corinthians 3. These are two kinds of veils. The veil in Hebrews 10 is the veil within the tabernacle (Heb. 9:3), but the veil in 2 Corinthians 3 is the veil upon Moses' face (v. 13). In type it was the veil upon Moses' face, but spiritually what is it? Probably very few have ever considered in a proper way what the veil is in this chapter. We need to be impressed that the veil is the religious traditions or the traditional religion. Why was there a veil covering the hearts of the sons of Israel when they read the

Old Testament? The veil on their hearts was the old, traditional religion.

We need to apply this understanding to ourselves. We always have a tendency to apply what we read in the Scriptures to others and not to ourselves. We may think that the Israelites in the Old Testament were foolish in many ways, and yet not realize that we are no different from them. You may have read the New Testament many times without seeing much light because you are veiled. You are covered with religious traditions, with Christian traditions. You are covered with traditional religion, with traditional Christianity. The background of Christianity may be a veil covering you. We have to realize that if we are going to live in the spirit, we have to be outside of religion, and we have to be delivered from all kinds of religious traditions. We need to go to the Lord in order to see our real situation. You may still be under the covering of the religious, traditional veil of Christianity. You may still be under the covering of the traditional teachings you received in the past. These all may have become a veil covering you from the real seeing of the Lord Himself.

The matter of religion is a real problem for those people who are seeking God. All day long many of the Lord's seekers are hindered and veiled by religion, which keeps them from seeing something of the Lord Himself. Judaism and Christianity with Catholicism and Protestantism have become great religious systems hindering the Lord's seekers from the experience and enjoyment of Christ as their life and everything. Religion is a device of the enemy. Who condemned the Lord Jesus to death? The Jewish religionists with the Old Testament in their hands. The religious people condemned and sentenced the Lord Jesus to death according to their understanding of the Old Testament. Who has persecuted the Lord's seekers throughout the history of the church? The religious people. Who persecuted the apostles? The Jewish religionists. Who persecuted Martin Luther? The Roman Catholics. Sometimes you may be your own persecutor because you are so religious. You have to be released and delivered from all traditional religion.

With a mirror there is the need of an unveiled face. There

is also the need for the mirror to be turned in the right direction. This is why 2 Corinthians 3:16 tells us that whenever the heart "turns to the Lord, the veil is taken away." Our heart needs to be turned to the Lord so we can behold Him with an unveiled face. You may feel that you have given up religion with all its traditions many years ago. You may have even left the denominations, but after that to whom did you turn? You may have turned in the wrong direction. A mirror has to be turned in the direction of your face to behold and reflect you. When the mirror turns to you, it reflects you. You may have given up traditional religion, but where is your direction? What are you after now? Are you directing yourself to the Lord Himself? Have you turned yourself to the Lord? We need to be unveiled and we need to be directed to the Lord Himself.

These verses in 2 Corinthians 3 should not merely be a doctrine to us. The real deliverance from traditional religion is not something merely outward, but it is something in the spirit. When you are really walking, working, acting, and behaving yourself in the spirit, you are out of religion and traditions. I doubt that many of us who have given up the way of denominations have been walking and living in the spirit since that time. If you have not been walking, living, acting, and behaving yourself in the spirit, you may have given up some traditions, but you are still living in your own traditions. You may have given up one religion only to form another one. Apart from the spirit, even you yourself become a religion.

To be delivered out of religion and out of tradition is to live, walk, act, and behave in the spirit. This is a matter that is very strict. If you are in the spirit, you are out of the denominations, out of the traditions, and out of any kind of religion. If you are not in the spirit, you may apparently be outside of religion, but you are actually still in your own religion. That religion is a veil covering you, so the Bible is not an open book to you. Your religion is a veil covering your eyes from seeing the light, the revelation, the visions in the New Testament. We have to turn ourselves from any kind of religion, even from the self-made religion. We have to turn ourselves to the Spirit.

Many dear saints have a self-made religion. A brother once came to tell us that he felt pray-reading the Word was not so right. He felt that we needed to worship the Lord in the way of everyone being quiet and praying slowly. This is a self-made religion. Another brother may feel that he must go out to the foreign field to be a missionary. This also may be a self-made religion. In the Far East, a British brother once asked me why the men sit together among themselves and the women sit together among themselves in our church meetings. He said that this was not the right way to meet. This is also a self-made religion. This religion immediately becomes a veil, veiling him from seeing Christ, veiling him from the real life in the Holy of Holies. Many of us may be unaware of the fact that we have our own self-made religion.

We all have to be delivered from the veil of religion. "The Lord is the Spirit, and where the Spirit of the Lord is, there is freedom" (2 Cor. 3:17). The Spirit frees us from any kind of religion. Worshipping the Lord is not a matter of separating the men from the women nor of mixing them together. John 4:24 tells us that we must worship God in spirit. We have to live in the spirit and meet the Lord in the spirit. I do not care how the saints sit in the meeting. I only care for one thing—whether or not I am in the spirit. The Lord is the Spirit in our spirit (2 Tim. 4:22; Rom. 8:16). If we keep ourselves in the spirit, the veil is gone immediately. We will have an unveiled face, not the outward physical face, but the inward spiritual face. We will be able to see the Lord, and others will see Him in us through our reflection of Him. We will become a beholding and reflecting mirror of Christ.

A man living in the spirit must be a captive of Christ, a letter of Christ, and a mirror turned to the Lord with an unveiled face. Then this man will behold and reflect the glory of the Lord, and he will be transformed dispositionally in his very being into the image of Christ from one degree of glory to another degree. This transformation proceeds from the Lord Spirit and has nothing to do with any religion, with any forms, with any regulations, with any different teachings, or with any dead knowledge. We have to turn ourselves to the spirit to contact the Lord Spirit with an unveiled face. To behold the Lord with an unveiled face is to be freed from all religion. As we solely take care of the Spirit living within us, day by day and hour after hour, we will be transformed into the same image of Christ.

A VESSEL, A CAMERA

Second Corinthians 4:7 says, "We have this treasure in earthen vessels." We are the vessels to Christ. As vessels we contain a wonderful treasure, the Christ of glory, who is the embodiment of God to be our life and our everything. If you read the first ten verses of chapter four carefully, you will realize that this vessel is exactly the same as a camera. Four main items needed for a camera to take any picture are the lens, the film, the shutter to open the camera, and the light. Through the light the scenery is brought into the camera and impressed on the film, producing a picture. Without the light, the scenery could never get into the camera. I once took a camera with me on a trip, and I took many pictures. When I had the film developed, the pictures were all blank. I wondered what happened. Eventually, I realized that I did not take away the lens cover.

In the spiritual realm, the mind with all the thoughts is the lens, and a right spirit in a right heart is the film within. You need to have an open mind with a right spirit in a right heart. Then you need the shutter, which means you need to open yourself to the Lord. The divine light is waiting for this. When you open yourself to the Lord, when your mind with the thoughts is open, and you have a right spirit in a right heart, the divine light brings Christ into your spirit and impresses Christ into your spirit. Now within you there is a picture, an image, and this image is the very treasure contained in these earthen vessels.

Our mind with our thoughts needs to be so open, and our heart needs to be right with a pure and proper spirit. Day and night we need to open ourselves to the Lord; then Christ, the heavenly, divine scenery, will be impressed into you again and again. Do not say that you have already been saved and that

Christ is in you already. Christ is in you, in your spirit, but He is not in your heart so much. You need again and again to have an open mind with all your thoughts regulated by Him, and you need a proper heart with a pure and open spirit. All day long you need to use the shutter, which means you need to open yourself to the Lord. Then Christ as the heavenly treasure will be impressed into you.

After we allow Christ to come into us, we need to be broken. The vessel needs to be broken that the treasure might be expressed. The first part of chapter four tells us how Christ as the treasure could come into us. Then the last part tells us how this treasure could be expressed by the vessel being broken. In verse 7 it says that "we have this treasure in earthen vessels, that the excellence of the power may be of God and not of us." Then in verses 8 through 10 you have words such as "afflicted", "perplexed", "persecuted", "cast down", and "always bearing about in the body the putting to death of Jesus". In verse 16 Paul tells us the outward man is decaying. This is not only the reducing of our outward man but also the breaking of the vessel.

God is doing a work not only to reduce us but also to crush us, to break us. We should not try to keep ourselves so complete, so whole. We have to be broken. The Lord wants to break our outward man, the natural man, including the soul and the flesh. Our human element, the soulish life, the fleshly element, all have to be broken. In a positive sense you are a camera with a lens, with the proper film, and with a shutter allowing the light to come in and bring the divine scenery, the divine image, into you. After this, however, you have to be prepared to be broken, to be crushed, to be destroyed. In the third chapter the problem is the veil. In the fourth chapter the problem is the outward man. The veil as we have seen is religion. The outward man is the self with the natural life, with the soulish life, and with the flesh. To know what the natural man, the flesh, and the soul are is one thing, but to experience the breaking of the outward man, the holy brokenness, is another thing.

In following the Lord, we should not expect that all the time we will have a "safe journey." In taking the way that leads to life, the narrow and constricted way to follow the Lord (Matt. 7:14), you will be afflicted, perplexed, persecuted, and cast down. You will be put to death, destroyed, crushed, broken. You may ask how this will happen. I do not know the way that this will take place. Only He knows. The Lord has myriads of ways to crush you and to crush me. One may say it is awful to get married. Then I would say that it is pitiful not to marry. Someone may ask whether it is better to marry or not to marry. I do not know. But I can tell you not to try to escape the Lord. The more you try to escape, the more you will be involved. If you escape from being afflicted, you will fall into being perplexed. If you escape from being persecuted, you will be cast down. We need to realize that we are not in our own hands. We are in His hands. No one knows what tomorrow may bring. Even David said in Psalm 31:15, "My times are in thy hand." We need to praise Him, however, that His hand is the sovereign hand, the gracious hand, and the merciful hand. We should not be afraid. We need to be at peace to take whatever He measures to us, to take whatever He assigns to us. Because we have the treasure within this vessel, the destiny for this vessel is to be broken.

To be a person in the spirit in the Holy of Holies, we need to be captives, letters, mirrors, and vessels to be broken. We need to bring all of these points to the Lord and pray thoroughly. We need to pray ourselves into these points so that we realize subjectively that we are rebellious captives, letters under the inscribing of the Spirit of the living God, mirrors with unveiled faces turned to Him, and vessels who are always under His dealing, under His breaking, to fulfill His burden to express the treasure within. All of these items are glorious. As a conclusion to the fellowship in this chapter, it would be helpful to sing and to pray *Hymns,* 403.

CHAPTER SIX

AMBASSADORS AND CO-WORKERS

Scripture Reading: 2 Cor. 5:4, 5, 9, 10, 13-17, 20; 6:1, 4-10

In this chapter we want to see the fifth and sixth aspects of a person who is living in the presence of the Lord, in the Holy of Holies. Thus far, we have seen that such a person is a captive, a letter, a mirror, and a vessel, a camera. The fifth and sixth aspects of such a person are an ambassador and a co-worker.

AN AMBASSADOR OF CHRIST

The Apostle Paul was an ambassador of Christ. An ambassador is one who represents the highest authority. The United States government has many ambassadors sent out to many different countries. These ambassadors represent the government of the United States. The highest authority in this universe is God, and God has given all the authority in heaven and on earth to Christ (Matt. 28:18). God has appointed Christ to be the King of kings, and the Lord of lords (1 Tim. 6:15; Rev. 17:14). Today Jesus is the Christ, the Lord of all, the highest authority. For this highest authority there is the need of some ambassadors on this earth who are qualified to represent Him. The Lord's ministry is not a matter of merely being a preacher or a teacher but of being one who is authorized with the heavenly authority, representing the highest authority in the whole universe. First, we need to be captured by Christ, and eventually we need to become a representative of Christ on this earth to deal with the earthly nations as an ambassador.

Some Christians have the title "Ambassador of Christ" printed on their witnessing card along with their name.

Many years ago I had a card that said "Bondslave of Christ—Witness Lee." At that time I did not dare to entitle myself an ambassador of Christ, but now I have a fuller realization that we all have to be ambassadors of Christ on this earth. We are not only the captives of Christ. Eventually, we have to be the ambassadors of Christ representing Him on this earth for all His interests. You may think that this is something too great, too big. Maybe some of the sisters would think that they are just the weak vessels. They may wonder how they could be the ambassadors of Christ, representing the highest authority on this earth. Regardless of whether you are a brother or a sister, all of us are members of the Body of Christ. The highest authority is Christ as the Head, and we as members of the Body have to be representatives of the Head. As a representative of the Head, you are an ambassador. Do not consider that you are little or that you are too weak. Being an ambassador is not a matter of whether you are little or weak. Actually, we have to be more weak, even weak in Christ (2 Cor. 13:4).

Not Living by What We Are or Can Do
But By the Immortal Life, Christ Himself

As an ambassador of Christ, Paul realized that whatever was within him, whatever he was, and whatever he had was mortal (5:4). Anything that is subject to death is mortal. Our wisdom is mortal, and our ability is mortal. Whatever we can do, whatever we are, and whatever we have is going to die. This is why we should not have any trust in what we are. We have to realize that we are mortal beings, but God has wrought into us something which is eternal, something which will never die, something which will last forever. Because we have received the Lord Jesus and He lives in us, we possess His immortal divinity. Eventually all that we are that is mortal will be "swallowed up by life" (5:4). Mortality will be swallowed up by the divine life.

If we are going to represent Christ on this earth as His ambassadors, we have to be clear that we are mortals, that whatever we can do, whatever we are, and whatever we have will die. We should not have any trust in ourselves nor should we live by ourselves. We need to realize that someone else is within us. This Person is the immortal life, the divine life (John 14:6). We should trust in this life, live by this life, and behave ourselves by this life. This life qualifies us and equips us to be the ambassadors of Christ. A person is not qualified to be an ambassador of Christ by power, by gift, or by knowledge, but by the immortal life within him. We need to forget about ourselves, to give up whatever we can do and whatever we are, and put our trust in this immortal life which is God Himself in Christ. This is the first qualification equipping us to be the ambassadors of Christ.

Ambitious to Please Christ

Since I realize that I have Christ as the immortal life within me, I have to endeavor with an ambition to please Him all the time (2 Cor. 5:9). If you are going to be an ambassador of Christ, there must be one day in this whole universe in which you make a decision, calling the heavens and the earth to be the witnesses, that you are now absolutely for Christ, that you only have one ambition—to please Christ. God has wrought Himself as the immortal life into us so that we should not live by ourselves but by this life. Now we have to be ambitious to please Him.

I do not want to say that you have to merely consecrate yourselves. Consecration is somewhat popular in today's Christianity. Many people in revival meetings may answer the call to come to the front and consecrate themselves. They may consecrate themselves and yet still be ambitious for themselves and not for Christ. Therefore, although they have consecrated themselves to Christ, they cannot represent Christ. We need to ask ourselves what our ambition is today. If we are going to represent Christ on this earth as His ambassadors, we should pray, "Lord, I call the heavens and the earth to witness that my ambition is one—just to please You."

Constrained by the Love of Christ

In 5:14 Paul says that "the love of Christ constrains us." Because the love of Christ constrained him, Paul was a person that lived to the Lord (v. 15). Another item which equips us to be the ambassadors of Christ is the constraining love of Christ. You must be a person carried away by the love of Christ. In 2 Corinthians 5:14-15 Paul tells us that the dying love of Christ is like the rushing of great waters toward us, impelling us to live to Him beyond our own control. To be constrained is similar to being carried away by a tide of water. The love of Christ is as strong as a tide of water which overcomes you and carries you away. We need to be flooded by the love of Christ. We need to be constrained by His love so that we have no choice. We should be able to say, "I have no other way to go. I have to love the Lord because His love has constrained me. What can I do?" When the flood waters come, you do not have a choice as to whether you will receive them or not. The flood waters give you no choice. We all have to be constrained by the love of Christ in such a way.

I must confess that I have prayed day by day for years that the Lord would show me His love that I could be constrained by the love of Christ. I prayed in this way—"Lord, constrain me with Your love. O Lord, flood me with Your love." All of us need to pray in this way. The young saints among us need to realize that although they love the Lord today, they are still at the crossroads of their Christian experience. There are many directions for them to choose, to take. You may have many choices, but once you are flooded by the love of Christ, you lose all the choices.

Knowing Others According to Christ in the Spirit

The fourth aspect of a person who is an ambassador is that he does not know people according to the flesh but according to Christ in the spirit. We should never consider anything or try to know a person by the outward appearance according to the flesh but always according to Christ in the spirit. Suppose that you hear a brother speak who is very eloquent, inspiring, and who has a great amount of knowledge. You may admire his eloquence and think that he gives marvelous messages. If you say this, this may mean that you recognize people or acknowledge things by the outward appearance according to the flesh and not by Christ according to the spirit. While you are listening to the speaking, you have to realize how much of God has been wrought into the speaker. You should not know him according to his eloquence, his knowledge, his gift, or according to what he teaches but according to the spirit. You have to realize whether or not there is something of Christ, of God, wrought into this person. Another brother may share without any eloquence, yet you realize that with him there is a weighty measure of Christ. This is why Paul said in 2 Corinthians 5:16, "So that we, from now on, know no one according to flesh; even if we have known Christ according to flesh, yet now we know Him so no longer." To recognize things and realize persons not according to the outward appearance in the flesh but according to the measure of Christ in the spirit is the fourth qualification of an ambassador of Christ.

The church needs a group of people who can practically represent Christ on this earth. If you are going to be such an ambassador, you should not live anymore by what you are or by what you can do. You have to live by the immortal life which is Christ Himself, and you have to be so ambitious to please Him. You also have to be flooded and carried away by the constraining love of Christ and learn how to recognize things, how to discern things, not by outward appearance but by the inward measure of Christ in the spirit. Then you will be the ambassador of Christ representing His authority and interest on this earth.

A CO-WORKER OF GOD

Bound together with God

The sixth aspect of a person who lives in the spirit, in the Holy of Holies, is that he is a co-worker of God (6:1). It is not an easy thing to be a co-worker to anyone. You may work together with others and yet still not be a co-worker. If two brothers are going to be co-workers, God has to bind them together. For two brothers to be co-workers is similar to binding their legs together so that together they have three legs instead of four. It is hard for people to run together in a three-legged race. If two brothers can work together in this way, they are co-workers or you could even call them "co-walkers."

To be a co-worker of God means you have to be bound with God. You have to lose something of yourself into Him. For one to merely be the Lord's servant is easier than being the Lord's co-worker. It may be easier to serve a brother than it is to be his co-worker. To be a co-worker causes much bondage. I may want to rise at six a.m., but the brother I am with wants to stay in bed until seven forty-five a.m. Since I am his co-worker, I have to wait for him. You may have the burden to go to Seattle, but the other brother may have the burden to stay in San Francisco. What shall you do? You cannot run away because you are bound to him. You are his co-worker.

A co-worker to God is one who is bound together with God. When God works, he works. When God walks, he walks. When God stops, he stops. You may be a diligent person who wants to do more work for God, but God may say, "I do not want you to do more work for Me right now; I want you to rest with Me. I am resting, so you have to rest with Me." So many so-called servants of the Lord simply cannot suffer resting together with the Lord. What the church needs is not a group of able workers but a group of people who are bound together with God, who are co-workers with God. When God works, you work. When God rests, you have to rest. When God withdraws, you withdraw. When God goes on, you go on. You do this because you are bound with Him as one.

The Signs of a Co-worker

Now we need to see the signs that prove that someone is a co-worker with God. Second Corinthians 6:4-10 gives us these signs. In 6:4-7a Paul lists eighteen qualifications of a minister of the new covenant: in much endurance, in afflictions, in necessities, in distresses, in stripes, in imprisonments, in tumults, in labors, in watchings, in fastings, in pureness, in knowledge, in longsuffering, in kindness, in a holy spirit, in unfeigned love, in the word of truth, and in the power of God. From the middle of verse 7 through verse 10 Paul speaks of three groups of things and seven kinds of persons. Paul said that he was commended as a minister of God through three groups of things—through the weapons of righteousness on the right and on the left, through glory and dishonor, and through evil report and good report (vv. 7-8). He was also commended as a minister of God in seven ways, as seven kinds of persons—"as deceivers and yet true, as unknown and well known, as dying and behold we live, as being disciplined and not being put to death, as made sorrowful yet always rejoicing, as poor yet enriching many, as having nothing and possessing all things" (vv. 8b-10). Verses 4 through 10 of chapter six show us the qualifications, the proofs, and the signs that a person is a co-worker of God.

Through Evil Report and Good Report

If you consider that you are a co-worker of God, you need to ask yourself whether or not there have been evil reports about you. Have you ever been evilly spoken of? If you have never been, I am afraid that you are not a co-worker of God. To be faithful to co-work with God causes people to speak evil about you. If you are really faithful to God and behave yourself as one with God, there will be many evil reports concerning you. Only a politician tries to please everyone. Many people may give a good report about a politician. But if you are a co-worker of God and are faithful to His aim, you will offend many people. When we were co-working with the Lord in Mainland China, some people would say, "They have a wonderful piece of work in China, but there is a 'dead fly in the ointment'." When you asked these ones what the dead fly in the ointment was, they had nothing definite to say.

The evil report comes from the opposers and the persecutors (Matt. 5:11). The good report comes from the believers and those who receive the truth preached and taught by the apostles. Through the years this has been our situation. We have received both evil reports and good reports. If you always receive only a good report, probably you are not honest and faithful to the Lord. If you are faithful to the Lord and honest with the church and saints, you will receive evil reports as well as good reports. Because you are co-working with God, you will receive the evil reports.

We need to learn to be faithful co-workers to God. We need to learn to suffer, to accept all these signs and proofs of being a co-worker with God. May the Lord raise up saints in many localities who are co-working with God. Through these people, God's interest will be taken care of on this earth.

CHAPTER SEVEN

THE TEMPLE
AND THE VIRGIN

Scripture Reading: 2 Cor. 6:14-18; 7:1; 11:2-4

THE TEMPLE OF GOD

In 2 Corinthians 6:14—7:1 we see the seventh aspect of a
person living in the Spirit—the temple of God. In these verses
Paul mentions some negative things that can defile the
temple of God. In verse 14 there are the unbelievers, lawlessness, and darkness. In verse 15 there is Belial, that is, Satan,
the Devil. Finally, in verse 16 there are the idols. These are
the five negative, unclean things which can defile the temple
of God. As the temple of God, we have to be separated from
these things. To say this is easy, but to put this matter of
separation into practice is not so easy. As a part of the temple
of God, you need to consider whether or not you are fully,
thoroughly separated from all these negative things. Have you
separated yourself from the unbelievers, from lawlessness,
from darkness, from the enemy Satan, and from anything
involving idols?

A captive needs to be captured; a letter needs to be written;
a mirror needs to be unveiled; a vessel needs to be broken;
and an ambassador needs to be absolutely on this earth for
the Lord's interest and under His authority. The ambassador
of the United States in Germany is there for the interest of
the United States and is fully under the authority of the
government of the United States. With a co-worker, there is
the need to be bound together with God. As the temple of God,
we need to be holy or separated. In 7:1 Paul said, "Therefore,

having these promises, beloved, let us cleanse ourselves from all defilement of flesh and spirit, perfecting holiness in the fear of God." The defilement of flesh and spirit in this verse refers to the five negative things mentioned in 6:14-16. Some of those items will defile your flesh while others will defile your spirit. The idols and Belial will defile your spirit, so you have to separate yourself, purify yourself, from all the negative things.

A dwelling place is always an expression of the dweller. When one looks at the inside of an American house, he can recognize that an American lives there. If you look at the residence of a Japanese, you will immediately know that a Japanese person lives there. This is because a dwelling place is always an expression of the dweller. Since we are the dwelling place of God, we should be the expression of God as the Dweller. You may say that you are a part of the temple of God and yet still be yoked together in something with an unbeliever. There may be some things with you which are very unrighteous and in darkness. Maybe you are involved with something connected with Belial or the idols. In order to be the temple of God in reality, we have to be separated absolutely and thoroughly that we may perfect holiness in the fear of God. If we consider that we are the dwelling place, the temple of God, and yet still hold on to something which is not corresponding to the nature or character of God, we are not perfecting holiness in the fear of God.

Holiness is separation unto God from all things other than Him. As the temple of God, we need to separate ourselves from anything which is against the divine nature, which is against the holy character of God. Perfecting holiness is to make this separation full and perfect, to have our entire being—spirit, soul, and body—fully and perfectly separated, sanctified unto God (1 Thes. 5:23). This is to be fully reconciled to God. Since we realize that we are the temple of God, we have to separate ourselves, to perfect holiness in the fear of God. We are afraid that if we do not do this, we will offend God and His shekinah glory will leave us.

A VIRGIN TO CHRIST

Paul told the Corinthians in 11:2, "I am jealous over you with a jealousy of God; for I betrothed you to one Husband, to present a pure virgin to Christ." All of the saints, especially the brothers, need to realize that they are a part of the virgin to Christ. Before the Lord and to the Lord we have to consider ourselves as females. We have to love the Lord just like a virgin loves her husband. A brother may be a husband, but to Christ he is a part of His wife. All the believers are the virgins, regardless of whether they are brothers or sisters (S. S. 1:3). We all are virgins and are a part of the corporate virgin to Christ. If you behave yourself as a man before Christ, this is wrong. If you do this, you insult the Lord's headship; you have to behave yourself as a virgin before the Lord. Not many brothers have the consideration that although they are men, they are a virgin to Christ. Paul betrothed the believers as a chaste, pure virgin to Christ.

In 11:3 Paul said, "I fear lest somehow, as the serpent deceived Eve by his craftiness, your thoughts should be corrupted from the singleness and the purity which is toward Christ." As a virgin we need to be pure and single or simple. Singleness in this verse can also be translated into simplicity, referring to the believers' single-hearted loyalty, single-minded faithfulness, toward Christ. For yourself as a virgin you need to be pure. For your husband, you need to be simple. Divorces are the issue of complexity. If the wives kept themselves in simplicity regarding their husbands, there would be no divorce. Once a woman gets married, she should be so simple regarding her husband. But many wives are seduced and tempted away from simplicity into complexity. A wife may consider her husband and realize that he is not so well-educated. But when she looks at another man, she realizes he is more educated. The more she compares her husband to other men, the more she realizes that he is not as good as them in certain aspects. In the past the serpent deceived Eve by his craftiness, and the same serpent is still deceiving so many Eves.

The apostles ministered Christ to people in a simple way.

Their teachings concerning Christ were very simple. Even Christ presented Himself in a simple way. In the Gospel of John He said that He was the door (10:1), the vine tree (15:1), and the bread of life (6:48). The Apostle Paul ministered Christ to others in a simple way, presenting Christ to them as their unique Husband. But some of the preachers during that time came to preach Christ in a complicated way. This is why Paul referred to those who preached "another Jesus" (2 Cor. 11:4). Because some were preaching Christ not in the way of simplicity but in the way of complexity, Paul was concerned for the Corinthians that their thoughts might be seduced or corrupted from the simplicity which is toward Christ. In the beginning God presented the tree of life to Adam and Eve in a very simple way (Gen. 2:9). Then the seducer, the tempter, the serpent, caused Eve to become complicated. With the tree of life there is only one element—life. The tree of life is simple, but the tree of the knowledge of good and evil with the element of death is complicated.

To follow the Lord, to walk in the spirit, to live in the Holy of Holies, we need to be so simple. Some came to me advising me not to teach others in such a simple way. They advised me to open people's eyes to see so many different kinds of teachings. When Adam and Eve ate of the tree of the knowledge of good and evil, the Bible tells us that "the eyes of them both were opened" (Gen. 3:7). The serpent even told Eve, "For God doth know that in the day ye eat thereof, then your eyes shall be opened, and ye shall be as gods, knowing good and evil" (Gen. 3:5). The eyes of Eve were really opened, showing us that it is better to have our eyes closed unto the simplicity which is toward Christ. We should have the attitude that we do not know anything except the simplicity concerning Christ being our Savior, our Lord, our life, our Husband, and our everything, concerning the church as the unique expression of Christ, and concerning the practice of the church life on the unique ground of oneness. This is so simple.

All of the different teachings, differing from the apostles' teaching centered upon Christ and the church, cause much complexity. This is why Paul urged Timothy to charge certain ones not to teach differently (1 Tim. 1:3). Many Christians do not know which direction to take because one "spiritual" person says one thing, and another "spiritual" person says another thing. The many different teachings in today's Christianity cause many seeking Christians to wonder who is right. We all need to learn to be somewhat foolish in our simplicity toward Christ. When I first began to travel to minister the word in Mainland China, I had a traveling library. One small suitcase was for my clothes, and a large trunk contained my books. The more I traveled for the Lord and in the Lord, however, the more books I dropped. Eventually, I traveled with only one book in my hand—the Bible. I liked to be so foolishly simple toward Christ.

We all need to learn to close our ears to the different teachings. Second Timothy 4:3-4 says, "For the time will come when they will not tolerate healthy teaching, but according to their own lusts they will heap up to themselves teachers tickling the ear, and they will turn away their ear from the truth, and will be turned aside to fables." The itching ear is the ear that seeks pleasing speaking for its own pleasure. The itching and turned-away ear is the main factor of the worsening decline in the churches. We should not have an itching ear, heaping up to ourselves teachers. Our eyes and ears need to be closed unto the simplicity toward Christ. We need to be in the spirit, standing on the genuine ground of oneness, following the Lord in a simple way as a virgin.

Once a woman marries a man, she should have no other considerations regarding her husband. She should only know that he is her husband and that he is the best among the best. She should be foolishly satisfied with her husband and blindly convinced that he is the best man for her. She should have the attitude that no other husband is as good as hers on the entire earth. If a woman is so simple in this way, she will have a sweet marriage life. The divorce rate is very high because the women today are not so simple toward their husbands. In like manner, we need to be simple toward Christ. We need to be blindly and foolishly satisfied with Him alone. We should not know anything but Christ and have the attitude that nothing is as good as Christ. He is the best, and we just love Him. For us there is only one tree—the tree of life. We would not consider the other tree with its complications.

Whenever you consider another husband other than Christ, you are out of the Holy of Holies, out of the spirit. When you would consider taking another way to practice the church besides the way revealed in the holy Word, you are out of the spirit. The more that we go on in the church life pursuing our dear Lord Jesus "blindly," the more we will be in the spirit, in the presence of the Lord, in the Holy of Holies, and the more we will be built up together with all the saints. When you have some consideration as to whether or not the practice of the church life revealed in the Bible is right, you are immediately in the wilderness and out of the spirit. You are in the soul, in the Holy Place, and out of the Holy of Holies, out of the land of Canaan. You are still wandering in the wilderness.

Some who took the way of the Lord's recovery had a good start, but at a certain point their minds, their thoughts, were corrupted from the singleness and the purity which is toward Christ. The serpent came to them in the form of a question mark in the same way that he came to Eve. The serpent asked Eve, "Hath God said, Ye shall not eat of every tree of the garden?" (Gen. 3:1). When we allow the serpent to put a question mark in us concerning what God has said, we are seduced, we are beguiled, and we are immediately out of the spirit. We all need to learn to be so simple with Christ. To follow the Lord, we all have to be simple. Paul was jealous over the believers with a jealousy of God that they would be so simple toward Christ as their one Husband.

We need to keep in mind the eight aspects we have covered of a person who is living in the spirit, in the Holy of Holies—a captive, a letter, a mirror, a vessel, an ambassador, a co-worker, a temple, and a virgin. As a captive, you need to be captured; as a letter, you need to be written; as a mirror, you need to be unveiled; as a vessel, you need to be broken; as an ambassador, you need to be wholly for His interest and under His authority; as a co-worker, you need to be bound; as a temple, you need to be separated to perfect holiness in the fear of God; and as a virgin, you need to be so simple. Learn to be simple, then you will be kept in the spirit.

CHAPTER EIGHT

LOVERS OF THE CHURCH AND TASTERS OF CHRIST

Scripture Reading: 2 Cor. 1:1; 11:28-29; 12:11-19, 7-10

Thus far, we have seen eight aspects of people who live and walk in the spirit in the presence of the Lord: captives, letters, mirrors, vessels, ambassadors, co-workers, the temple, and the virgin. In this chapter we want to see the last two aspects of such people—lovers of the church and tasters of Christ.

LOVERS OF THE CHURCH

If we have really been captured by the Lord, are under His writing in the spirit, are unveiled mirrors reflecting Him all the time, are broken vessels to express Him, mean business with Him to represent Him on this earth as His ambassadors, are bound with Him as one to be His co-workers, are the temple for His rest, and are the virgins to Him for His satisfaction, we are surely lovers of the church because the Body of Christ, the church, is what Christ is longing for. Nothing is so precious in the Lord's eyes, in the Lord's feelings, as the church. Ephesians 5 tells us that Christ loved the church to such an extent that He gave Himself up for her (v. 25). Some Christians would say that we should not consider the church so much. They feel that we should be careful not to consider the church more than Christ and not to make the church an idol to ourselves. But if we know what the church is and if we love the Lord and realize what His heart's desire is, we will love the church more and more than ever before. Today the Lord is for nothing but the church. He desires the church, His Body, to express Him on this earth today among the human race. The church is not something in the future and not something merely in the heavenlies. In the future and in the heavenlies there will be no problems to overcome. But today here on this earth we need to overcome all the problems to realize what the church life is that we may fulfill the Lord's heart's desire. Second Corinthians shows us that the Apostle Paul's heart was fully for the church and on the church. The church was so precious to him because he realized what the Lord's heart's desire is.

Second Corinthians was not addressed to individual saints but to the church of God (1:1). It was not addressed to the church in the heavenlies but to a local church in Corinth. In 1:1 Paul said, "To the church of God which is in Corinth, with all the saints who are in the whole of Achaia." Paul used the expression "with all the saints" not "and all the saints." We need to see the difference between these two expressions. To use the conjunction "and" means that the church and the saints are two separate entities, but to use "with" means that the church includes the saints. The saints belong to the church. If you are not one with the church, you are not qualified to receive this Epistle. For you to receive this book, you have to be in the position of being with the church. Second Corinthians was not written to any individual. We have seen that the temple is a corporate temple and that Paul betrothed the believers as one corporate virgin to Christ. If you are not with the church, you have no position to receive what is in 2 Corinthians because the entire book is written to the church with the saints. A letter may be written to a school with the students but not to the school and the students individually. The students do not have the position to receive this letter if they are not with the school.

Paul's letter was addressed to the church in a certain city on this earth not to the church in the heavenlies. You may say that you are with a church, but are you with an abstract, unseen, invisible church in the heavenlies or with a concrete, visible, practical local church today on this earth in the very place where you are? Many people who talk about the church are churchless. They are talking about a wonderful home in the future in the heavenlies, but today they are homeless.

All the Epistles written by the apostles were dealing with the local churches on the earth. All of us need to be in a local church where we can practice the proper Christian life today. The Apostle Paul was a pattern of a lover of the church. The church in Corinth spoke evil concerning Paul behind his back. They said he was crafty in making gain, indemnifying himself by sending Titus to receive the collection for the poor saints (12:16). If the brothers in your locality were to say that you were crafty and that you caught them by guile, you might want to leave that locality. If you did leave, this would mean that you are not a real lover of the church. Despite the Corinthians speaking such an evil word about him, Paul still loved them. In 12:15 he said, "But I will most gladly spend and be utterly spent on behalf of your souls, even if loving you more abundantly, I am loved less." For Paul to spend was to spend what he had, referring to his possessions. For him to be spent was to spend what he was, referring to his being. Paul was very frank, pure, and sincere, yet the church to whom he ministered said that he was crafty. He was not happy with this, but he was not offended. He still loved the church.

A real, proper mother could be unhappy with her children, but she would not be offended and leave them because she loves them. If we would be those following Paul, who is a pattern of the believers (1 Tim. 1:16), we have to love the church in spite of the way that we are treated by the church. If the church in your locality treated you in a bad way, it would be easy for you to have the attitude to withdraw from the church. Some saints do not come to the church meetings because they are offended by a certain brother. This shows that you have never seen what the church, the Body of Christ, is. You have never seen what the local expression of the Body is. If you do see this, you would never be offended because of the way the church treats you. You would still love the church. It may be that the more you love the church, the less the church returns to you. You may feel that you are "losing face" to continue meeting and going on with the church in your locality. This shows that you are not a church lover but that you love to save your own face. If you loved the church, you would not consider how to save your face. If you have the vision concerning the local expression of the Body of Christ on this earth in the place where you are, you will never be offended by the church.

In 1942 almost the entire church where Brother Watchman Nee was rose up against him. Some brothers came to Brother Nee suggesting that they begin to meet in other places since the saints treated him in such a poor way. Brother Nee told these brothers that if the church treated him well, it is the church, and if the church did not treat him so well, it is still the church. He charged these brothers to meet with the church and go on with the church regardless of how the church treated him. I can testify before the Lord that Brother Nee still loved the church during this time. He did many things secretly to help the church, which was so much against him. Praise the Lord that after six years, in 1948, the whole church repented to him. If you love the church, you would love it regardless of how it treats you simply because it is the expression of the Body of Christ.

The Apostle Paul said that he was so glad to spend whatever he had and whatever he was. He loved the church to such an extent. If we do not love the church as the Apostle Paul did, we actually have no position to talk about the church. If you are going to practice the church life and you do mean business with the Lord, you have to love the church with all that you have and with all that you are. You have to spend all that you have and all that you are on the church and for the church. May the Lord be gracious and merciful to us. If we mean business with the Lord in having a local expression of His Body, we cannot have it in a way of indifference. We should be able to tell the Lord that we love His Body more than ourselves. If you are this kind of person, you are in a position to talk about the church. We do not need theoretical teachings concerning the church, but we need the practical life of the church.

One brother I know of, who came to know the local expression of the Body of Christ, would spend all his time for the church life, using just enough of his time to make a living for himself and his family. This brother and his wife were wholly loving the church. They were willing to spend everything for the church and be spent. We should not be vain talkers concerning the church life, but we need to be involved in the practical life of the church. Do we really mean business to practice the church life on this earth today, or are we just talkers about some wonderful teachings concerning the church with no practicality? If we mean business with the Lord, we have to love the church with every drop of our blood. Paul was willing to spend and be spent on behalf of the church in Corinth in spite of the fact that the more he loved them, the less they loved him. This brother was a pattern as a lover of the church.

In 11:28 Paul said, "Apart from the things which are not mentioned, the pressure upon me daily, the anxiety for all the churches." Pressure in this verse literally means the "crowd (of cares) pressing on me." Paul loved all the churches in all the different cities. He had a real care and a sincere anxiety for all of them. If we want 2 Corinthians to be our experience, we must be one with the church and love it unconditionally.

TASTERS OF CHRIST

The tenth aspect of a person living in the spirit is that he is a taster of Christ. If we are going to love the church, we have to experience Christ. We have to be the tasters of Christ. Then we will have something of Christ to minister to the church which we love. In 2 Corinthians there is the aspect of loving the church and even more the aspect of tasting Christ, enjoying Christ, experiencing Christ. Paul received many visions and revelations; he tells us that he was "caught away to the third heaven" (12:2) and that he was "caught away into paradise" (v. 4). As a man living on earth, the apostle knew the things of the earth. But men do not know the things either in the heavens or in paradise, the pleasant part of Hades (Luke 23:43; 16:23, 25). However, the apostle was brought away to both of these unknown places. Hence, he received visions and revelations of these hidden regions. For this reason he mentions these two uttermost parts of the universe.

These visions and revelations, however, did not qualify Paul to be a lover of the church. It is not the visions and revelations that qualify us to be a lover of the church, but the experience, the tasting, the enjoyment of Christ. After he had received the visions and revelations, Paul said, "That I should not be exceedingly lifted up by the transcendence of the revelations, there was given to me a thorn in the flesh, a messenger of Satan, that he might buffet me, that I should not be exceedingly lifted up" (12:7). Paul asked the Lord three times to take away the thorn in his flesh. The Lord would not take the thorn away, however, in order that Paul might taste or enjoy Him as grace and experience His power. The Lord's reply to Paul was, "My grace is sufficient for you, for My power is perfected in weakness" (12:9). This was not a vision or a revelation but experience.

Today what the Body of Christ needs is not a group of people who merely have the visions and the revelations, but who have the practical experience of Christ. The Body needs those who enjoy Christ, who taste Christ, in a very experiential way. It is through this experience that we have something of Christ practically to minister to His Body. Revelations and visions alone will not work. The Apostle Paul had the visions, yet he had to be put "into the oven." If you say that you have the visions and the revelations, be prepared to be put into the oven. Sufferings and trials are often in the Lord's ordination for us, that we may experience Christ as grace and power. The Lord allows a thorn to come upon us so that we may experience the power of Christ in our weakness.

Today the church needs a group of brothers and sisters who are under the pressure, the thorn, to experience Christ in a practical way. We need to experience Him as the all-sufficient grace meeting our need in every kind of environment, and we need to taste Him, experiencing His power being perfected in our weakness. To magnify the sufficiency of the Lord's grace, our sufferings are required; to show forth the perfectness of the Lord's power, our weakness is needed. It is through our experience of Christ as grace and power that we will have something real of Christ to minister to His Body, which we love. If we are lovers of the church, we have to be the tasters of Christ. Otherwise, we will have nothing to minister to the church. What we have to minister to the church is only the very Christ whom we have enjoyed, whom we have experienced. We need the practical experience of Christ in the midst of our suffering. The ministry is constituted with, and produced and formed by, the experiences of the riches of Christ through sufferings, consuming pressures, and the killing work of the cross.

CHAPTER NINE

THE SPIRIT OF PAUL

Scripture Reading: 2 Cor. 6:11-13; 7:2-4, 12-16; 10:1-2, 7-12; 11:1, 5-31; 12:1, 11-19

If we read the verses above carefully again and again, we can see what kind of spirit this man, the Apostle Paul, had. Paul wrote fourteen Epistles in the New Testament, but not one of these Epistles gives us a picture of Paul's spirit in the way that 2 Corinthians does. As we have pointed out already, 2 Corinthians can be considered as an autobiography of the Apostle Paul. In this chapter I want to point out what kind of spirit the Apostle Paul had when he was serving the church. I am not referring to Paul's attitude, thinking, knowledge, or emotions but to his spirit. Our spirit is the deepest part of our being. It may also be considered as the genuine, real part of our being. A genuine man is a man in the spirit. We may be kind to others, but we are kind falsely because we are kind in the soul, not in the spirit. Sometimes we love others but we love them falsely because we love them in our soul, not in the spirit. When we do things in our spirit, we are real and genuine because our real man, our real being, is in the spirit. Sometimes we talk with people in the soul, not in the spirit. When we speak in this way, we are merely saying something to fit the situation and our talk is worldly. When we speak to others in the spirit, we are real and genuine. In this chapter we want to see nine aspects of the wonderful spirit of Paul. I am not referring to the Holy Spirit but to the human spirit of Paul (Acts 17:16; 19:21; Rom. 1:9; 2 Cor. 2:13).

AN OPEN SPIRIT

Based on the Scripture reading, the first characteristic,

the first virtue, of the spirit of this writer is its openness. This man Paul has an open spirit. It is not easy to have an open spirit. On the contrary, it is easy for us to close our spirit, to shut our spirit up. It could be that most of the time we are closed in our spirit. The more we are fallen, the more we are closed in our spirit; the more we are delivered, the more we are saved, the more we are open in the spirit. For the church life we need an open spirit.

You may open your mind, open your emotion, and even open your entire heart, yet you would still not open your spirit to others. When you open your spirit, you are fully, thoroughly open to others. In today's society, hardly any person is open to another person. They are open to one another at most in the soul, not in the spirit. Among the Christians it may be the same. For the church building, for the church life, we have to be open to one another in the spirit. I have to open to you in the spirit, but this needs the Lord's grace and this needs the working of the cross. Our natural man has to be broken; then we will be open in the spirit one to another.

Are you really open in your spirit and from your spirit to the brothers? Although this is not easy, there is the need of such an openness in our spirit toward others. It was not so easy for the Apostle Paul to be open in his spirit to the Corinthian believers. When you are welcomed by a group of people, it is easy for you to be open in the spirit to them. When you are criticized, opposed, and looked down on by others, however, you will become as closed as "a snail." You will withdraw your whole being into a "hard shell" and hide yourself there. When others criticize you, you remain in the shell. When others welcome you, you will come out to greet them. The shell into which we withdraw when others despise and criticize us is the shell of the self. When we withdraw into this shell, no one can touch us. If the members in a local church are all "snails," how can the church building be prevailing? For the Lord's sake and for the building up of the church, we all have to be open one with another. We have to open ourselves to the other members. I have never seen two snails working together. Every snail is individualistic. There is the need of the divine breaking to break the shell of the self so that we all may have open spirits.

A FRANK SPIRIT

The verses in the Scripture reading also show us that Paul was a man with a frank spirit. Today in the church it is difficult to see some brothers who are really frank. I have met some so-called spiritual people who spoke well concerning me to my face, but eventually I discovered that they spoke about me behind my back in a very bad way. This is not frank. In the church life we should not lose our temper, but we have to be frank with one another. We should not be political in the church life, but should always say something to a brother's face. We should not be backbiters (Rom. 1:30; Gal. 5:15). The Apostle Paul was a frank person with a frank spirit, and we need to be the same. Sometimes when you would be frank with others, they would think that you are mad with them. In today's American society people have learned to be political. Even some Christian ministers and Christian teachers have become politicians. They may highly appraise a person to his face, and yet speak something behind his back. This is something devilish. In the church life we should not be angry with one another. Anger does not accomplish anything for the Lord, but we have to be frank.

When you see that I am wrong in a certain matter, you have to tell me frankly in love, in a proper spirit. One brother may even come to another brother to ask him if he is wrong in a certain matter. If the other brother replies that he is not wrong and then behind his back speaks evil things concerning him, he is like "a serpent with two tongues." You should not speak behind someone's back what you cannot speak to his face. If your spirit does not allow you to say something, you should not say it. If you say something, you should say it truthfully, frankly. Paul was so frank that he even told the Corinthians, "I have become foolish; you yourselves compelled me. For I ought to have been commended by you" (12:11). We have to get rid of all the elements of the cunning serpent within us. In the local expression of the church, of the Body of Christ, we all have to be so faithful and frank. If I am wrong, tell me that I am wrong in love. Otherwise, you should not say anything.

A PURE SPIRIT

The Apostle Paul was also one who had a pure spirit. If you never say anything, it is easy for others to think that you are pure. But once you begin to speak, either your purity or lack of purity becomes manifested. In 2 Corinthians the Apostle Paul opened himself up and spoke many things, yet we are impressed with how pure his spirit is. We may now be clear that we have to be frank, but if we are going to be frank we have to be pure. A frank spirit has to be matched with a pure spirit. If you are not pure, your frankness will damage me. If I come to tell a brother that he is wrong in certain things, I have to test myself—is my spirit pure? If it is not pure, I should not be frank and I could not be frank. I have to be frank with a pure motive. To speak to a brother with a pure spirit edifies. Otherwise, if you are frank without purity, you will damage and destroy the saints. In the church life, we need such a frank and pure spirit.

A BOLD SPIRIT

Paul also had a bold spirit. In American slang we would say that Paul was not a "chicken." He was like a tiger. He told the Corinthians, "I have previously said as present the second time, and I say beforehand, being absent now, to those who have sinned before and to all the rest, that if I come again I will not spare" (13:2). This is a real servant of Christ. We need to have a bold spirit, not a timid spirit. This is why Paul told Timothy that "God has not given us a spirit of cowardice" (2 Tim. 1:7).

A HUMBLE SPIRIT

Paul's spirit was bold and yet it was also humble. If your spirit is bold and yet not humble, that is dangerous. You may kill all the brothers because you are so bold. Boldness needs the balance of humility. On the one hand, you have to be bold; on the other hand, you have to be humble. We are either very bold or very humble. When we are bold we do not know what humility is, and when we are humble we do not know what boldness is. We are like the unturned cake referred to in Hosea 7:8. These characteristics of humility and boldness in our spirit are necessary for the church life. Sometimes the sisters are keener than the brothers in noticing things that are wrong. They have this ability to see what is wrong and what is off, but most of the time they are not bold. They found out that something was wrong but they dared not tell the brothers. They used the excuse that they are the weaker vessels (1 Pet. 3:7). To be humble is proper, but sometimes the sisters have to exercise a bold spirit. There was a certain sister who was a co-worker who saw certain mistakes that the brothers did not see, and she would come to us with boldness with tears on her face. She said, "Brothers, I have to fellowship with you because we are wrong in a certain thing. Though I am a sister under the covering, I have to say this." Many times her fellowship became a deliverance from the Lord for us. This shows us that we need a bold spirit with humility and a humble spirit with boldness.

A LOVING SPIRIT

Paul spoke bold words, but his words were full of a loving spirit. Paul's spirit was a loving spirit, a spirit always stretching out to love others, to take care of others. I do not mean that we need a love which has its source in our emotions, but we need a loving spirit, a spirit within us that always loves others. The reason why I would be so frank to you in my spirit is because there is a lot of love in my spirit for you. What a person says with his words may be very different from his spirit. Someone may say that he loves you, but by discerning his spirit you know that he really does not love you. On the other hand, someone may tell you that he does not like you, but you realize that he loves you in his spirit. Many times mothers tell their children that they do not like them and they get upset with their children, but the children know that the mother loves them. A person's words may be loving but his spirit is not. We have to learn to know the spirit. Whether I highly appraise you or say something to rebuke you, you have to discern my spirit not just my words. For the building up of the church life, there is the need of such a loving spirit.

A TENDER SPIRIT

Another characteristic of Paul's spirit is that his spirit was tender. You can speak boldly in words, yet still with a tender spirit. We need to be dealt with by the working of the cross so that we can be a person with a tender spirit like the Apostle Paul.

A SPIRIT THAT IS NOT SELF-SEEKING

Paul's spirit was not self-seeking. Second Corinthians shows us that he had a spirit that never sought anything for himself. He had a spirit fully, wholly, and thoroughly delivered out of the self. Whatever his spirit sought was for the good of the church and for the interest of Christ. Such a spirit is greatly needed in today's church life. Whether or not the church in our place will be built up adequately depends upon our being a person with a spirit possessing all these characteristics. If we all would look to the Lord for His help in His grace to have the same spirit as the Apostle Paul, spontaneously the church life would be built up. We need a spirit that does not seek anything for the self.

A COORDINATING SPIRIT

The final characteristic of Paul's spirit is that his spirit was always coordinating with others. Our spirit might be tender, pure, and loving, yet not so cooperating or coordinating with other saints. The verses in the Scripture reading show us that Paul's spirit was always coordinating with his co-workers, coordinating with the local churches, and even coordinating with those believers who did not treat him so well. He was coordinating all the time, trying to be one with the saints, one with the local churches, and one with the co-workers. He was so coordinating in the spirit.

In this chapter we have seen nine aspects of this man's spirit: his spirit was open, frank, pure, bold, humble, loving, tender, not self-seeking, but coordinating. It would be helpful to pray-read all the verses in the Scripture reading with these nine points in mind. The more you pray-read all these verses, the more you will see that these nine points are so significant. These are the real characteristics of a person's spirit who lives in the Holy of Holies. We need such a spirit for the building up of the Lord's Body. Without such a balanced, adjusted spirit, the church life could never be realized by you regardless of how many doctrines and how much knowledge you possess. For us to realize the church life, we need such a balanced and adjusted spirit. May we all look to the Lord that we may have such a spirit.

CHAPTER TEN

CHRIST AS GRACE

Scripture Reading: 2 Cor. 1:12; 4:15; 6:1; 8:1, 2, 9; 9:8, 14, 15;
12:9; 13:14; John 1:14, 16-17; I Cor. 15:10; Gal. 6:18

HYMNS, 497

Grace in its highest definition is
God in the Son to be enjoyed by us;
It is not only something done or giv'n,
But God Himself, our portion glorious.

God is incarnate in the flesh that we
Him may receive, experience ourself;
This is the grace which we receive of God,
Which comes thru Christ and which is
  Christ Himself.

Paul the Apostle counted all as dung,
'Twas only God in Christ he counted grace;
'Tis by this grace—the Lord experienced—
That he surpassed the others in the race.

It is this grace—Christ as our inward strength—
Which with His all-sufficiency doth fill;
It is this grace which in our spirit is,
There energizing, working out God's will.

This grace, which is the living Christ Himself;
Is what we need and must experience;
Lord, may we know this grace and by it live,
Thyself increasingly as grace to sense.

CHRIST AS THE GOOD LAND

At the beginning of this book we pointed out that there are three major types in the Bible portraying the way by which God fulfills His purpose. These types are the good land of Canaan, the temple, and the bride. We have seen that the people who are living in the presence of God, in the shekinah glory of God, are the temple for God's rest and the virgins for Christ's satisfaction. In this chapter we want to see the all-inclusive type of Christ—the good land. We have to see how Christ as the grace of God is the very good land for us to enter into, to enjoy, to experience, to partake of, and to possess.

In 2 Corinthians we have the terms of the temple and the virgin but not the term of the good land. How could we say then that Christ is the good land for our enjoyment in 2 Corinthians? We have to realize that in 2 Corinthians we see a group of people who have attained to the uttermost to fulfill God's purpose. In 1 Corinthians Paul likened the Corinthians to the children of Israel. They had left Egypt by experiencing Christ as the Passover (1 Cor. 5:7), and they were wandering in the wilderness, experiencing Christ as the heavenly manna and as the spiritual Rock that flowed out the living water (1 Cor. 10:3-4). But there is no reference in 1 Corinthians to the good land of Canaan which the children of Israel eventually entered into and possessed. Where is the record of entering into the good land? It is in 2 Corinthians. Although the term of the good land is not used in this book, spiritually speaking we can see the good land in 2 Corinthians. The good land in this book is Christ Himself as the very embodiment of the processed Triune God given to us as the divine grace for our enjoyment. In this book we see some persons who possessed Christ as their God-given portion. These persons entered into the land promised and given by God, and they were enjoying this land, which is Christ Himself.

CHRIST AS GRACE

In this book Christ is the grace. In 13:14 Paul says, "The grace of the Lord Jesus Christ, and the love of God, and the fellowship of the Holy Spirit be with you all." According to the proper sequence, the love of God should be first. Here the grace of the Lord is mentioned first because 2 Corinthians is on the grace of Christ (1:12; 4:15; 6:1; 8:1, 9; 9:8, 14; 12:9). The grace of the Lord is the central thought, the subject of this book. In 12:9 the Lord told Paul that His grace was sufficient for him.

It may be that the term grace is quite familiar to us, but we may have a very shallow understanding of this term. Many Christians consider that grace is unmerited favor, something given to us by the Lord freely. I have no objection to this. For instance, Christ's dying on the cross for our sins is something done for us freely. Undoubtedly, this is really grace. Forgiveness and justification are things given by God to us which are of grace. But we must see that the New Testament shows us that mainly grace is nothing less than Christ Himself (1 Cor. 15:10; cf. Gal. 2:20) as the very embodiment of the processed Triune God for our enjoyment. Christ has come not merely to do something for us objectively, not merely to bring some good things from God to us freely. The purpose of the work of Christ is that He could come into us. His dying on the cross is not the purpose but the means to fulfill the purpose of Him coming into us for our enjoyment that we may enjoy Him as our life, our life supply, our strength, and our everything. Grace is Christ coming into us as our full enjoyment.

In 8:1 Paul said, "Furthermore, we make known to you, brothers, the grace of God which has been given in the churches of Macedonia." We might think that the grace given means that many good things were given to them by God, but the next verse shows us what this grace was. "That in much approvedness of affliction the abundance of their joy and the depth of their poverty abounded unto the riches of their liberality" (v. 2). The grace was not something given to them, but it was that they had the strength, the energy, to give something to others while they were so poor. In poverty and affliction they were willing and able to give something to others. This is grace. It may be that when we receive something given by God through others that we would say, "Praise the Lord, this is a great grace." Actually, this is childish talk. If you are mature in the divine life, you will realize that the greatest grace is not that you receive something but that there is Someone within you energizing you and enabling you to give something to others. Grace is not something received outwardly but Someone within, energizing, enabling, and strengthening us to do something for the Lord.

Another good example of grace is in chapter twelve. In verses 7 through 9 Paul said, "There was given to me a thorn in the flesh, a messenger of Satan, that he might buffet me, that I should not be exceedingly lifted up. Concerning this I entreated the Lord three times that it might depart from me. And He has said to me, My grace is sufficient for you." We might think that if the thorn were taken away, that would be a real grace. If you had some illness, you might ask the Lord to heal you, to take away your illness. If your illness were gone the next day, you would be excited, praising the Lord for His grace. But this is not the grace mentioned in 2 Corinthians. The grace that Paul experienced was related to a thorn in the flesh which troubled and buffeted him all the time. The Lord was not willing to take the thorn away but told Paul that His grace was sufficient. If we were Paul, we might have argued with the Lord—"Lord, if Your grace is sufficient, it has to be sufficient to take the thorn away." However, if the thorn is taken away, you can never experience the sufficient grace. You could never taste how sufficient this grace is. The grace mentioned here is not something done by the Lord or given by the Lord. It is simply the Lord Himself within you, supporting you, energizing you, and strengthening you to face the trouble, to meet the situation. This is a living grace, a real grace, and is nothing less than Christ as the very embodiment of the fullness of the Godhead (Col. 2:9) for our enjoyment.

I have seen a number of dear sisters who really loved the Lord, yet their husband would not go along with them. It seemed that the more they prayed for their husband, the more their husband became worldly. At first I could not understand the reason for this. Eventually, I found out that the more these dear sisters were troubled, bothered, and perplexed by their husband, the more they knew the Lord and the more they experienced the Lord as their grace. Whenever they opened their mouth to speak just a little bit, in their presence you had the sense that the Lord was there. Our human understanding cannot realize this because the divine thought, the divine concept, is very much different from ours. We hope that certain things might be accomplished by the Lord for us by "His grace." Eventually, however, nothing is done. Nothing is accomplished. Your environment and your situation does not change. You may say that you are fully disappointed, but it may be that you are still not disappointed enough. You may need to be disappointed more until you learn how to experience the grace of the Lord. We need to learn not to expect to receive anything outwardly or to have anything done by the Lord for us but just to enjoy the Lord Himself as the grace of God.

God assigned one particular co-worker that I knew another co-worker who was to him peculiar and troubling. He asked the Lord many times to be gracious and merciful to him so that he would not have to work with this brother. After many years, there was no answer to this prayer, no taking away of his fellow-worker. Eventually this brother was subdued by the Lord and realized that he had to accept this thorn. Then he prayed, "Lord, how I thank You for this precious, dear thorn upon me. Through this I can experience You more and more as my grace." He learned the lesson of how to enjoy the living Christ as grace, the embodiment of all the fullness of the Godhead within us for our enjoyment.

Out of the enjoyment of Christ Himself as grace comes forth the Body of Christ. The Body of Christ cannot come forth, cannot be brought into our practical experience, by teachings alone. The practical life of the Body of Christ could only come forth out of the enjoyment of Christ as the grace of God. The more we enjoy Him, the more we will possess of Him. Out of this possession of Christ as our grace the practical church life will be produced.

The temple, the building of God, for God's rest, for God's expression, and the virgin for Christ's satisfaction come forth out of the enjoyment of Christ as the grace of God, which is typified by the good land of Canaan. The grace of Christ is the enjoyment of the land. When we enjoy Christ as the grace of God, we are enjoying the riches of the good land. As we enjoy the unsearchable riches of Christ (Eph. 3:8), He will be wrought into us. Then our whole being will be thoroughly saturated with all the elements of Christ as we enjoy Him day by day. Out of this inward enjoyment and possession of Christ comes forth the building of the Body which is the virgin, the bride to Christ, for His satisfaction and the temple, the dwelling place of God, for His rest. The practical church life cannot be realized merely by teachings or visions but by the enjoyment of Christ as the grace of God.

THE WAY TO ENJOY CHRIST AS GRACE

We must have a bird's-eye view of the entire book of 2 Corinthians so that we can see the way to enjoy Christ. Some would answer that to enjoy Christ we need to pray-read the Word and exercise the spirit. This is true, but to really enjoy Christ in a rich way we must be the persons that are symbolized by the ten aspects that we have seen in the preceding chapters. We have to be captives, letters, mirrors, vessels, ambassadors, co-workers, a temple, a virgin, lovers of the church, and tasters of Christ. If we are going to enjoy Christ, we must be captured, conquered, and subdued by Him. Regardless of how much we try to exercise our spirit, if we are not captives of Christ, it will be hard for us to enjoy much of Christ as grace. The exercise of the spirit and pray-reading may not help you much because you are not yet subdued or captured by Christ. You also have to be a letter under His writing all the time in the spirit. As a mirror you have to be unveiled from religion with all of its traditions to behold and reflect the Lord. Then you need to be a vessel, on the one hand, to contain Him and to receive Him into you again and again, and on the other hand, to be broken, reduced, consumed all the time. You have to be an ambassador under His authority, representing Him for His interest on this earth, and you have to be a co-worker bound together with Him as one. There should be no more freedom and no more separation between you and the Lord. Then you will be a temple, wholly, thoroughly, and ultimately separated unto Him to perfect holiness in the fear of God. You also need to be a pure, chaste, and simple virgin to satisfy Him and spontaneously you will be a lover of the church of which you are a member. You will love the church unconditionally regardless of how the church treats you. Finally, you need to be the taster of Christ all the time. By all these aspects, we can enjoy Christ. If we have all these aspects, whenever we exercise our spirit, we will taste Christ. Whenever we pray-read the Word, we will take into us the sweet foretaste of Christ. This is the message of 2 Corinthians.

THE DIVINE TRINITY TRANSMITTED
INTO US FOR OUR ENJOYMENT

At the end of this Epistle Paul wrote, "The grace of the Lord Jesus Christ, and the love of God, and the fellowship of the Holy Spirit be with you all" (13:14). The three of the Godhead are one and love, grace, and fellowship are not three separate matters, but three aspects of one thing. God the Father is in Christ (John 14:10) and Christ is the Spirit (1 Cor. 15:45; 2 Cor. 3:17). Likewise, the love of God is in the grace of Christ, and the grace of Christ with the love of God is in the fellowship of the Holy Spirit. The love of God is the source, since God is the origin; the grace of the Lord is the course of the love of God, since the Lord is the expression of God; and the fellowship of the Spirit is the impartation of the grace of the Lord with the love of God, since the Spirit is the transmission of the Lord with God for our experience and enjoyment of the Triune God—the Father, the Son, and the Holy Spirit, with their divine virtues. The fellowship of the Holy Spirit transmits the grace of Christ with the love of God in it into us.

This is why Galatians 6:18 says, "The grace of our Lord Jesus Christ be with your spirit, brothers. Amen." God is in Christ, Christ is the Spirit, and the Spirit is in our spirit for our enjoyment. God to us is the love, Christ to us is the grace, and the Spirit to us is the fellowship, the transmission, transmitting all that Christ is as grace, with all that God is as love in Him, into us for our enjoyment. All that God is in His Trinity is now being transmitted into us for our enjoyment. This is the good land, the rich land, flowing with milk and honey with all the riches of the processed Triune God. These riches for our enjoyment include the love of God, the grace of Christ, and the transmission of the Holy Spirit for our experience.

I hope that we can bring all this fellowship to the Lord in prayer that we all might be brought into the realization of the riches of Christ in 2 Corinthians. Then there will be a living expression of the Body of Christ in many localities by the experience of Christ. Praise Him! He is the grace as the good land for our enjoyment to produce the temple for God's rest and the virgin for Christ's satisfaction.

ABOUT THE AUTHOR

Witness Lee was born in 1905 in northern China and raised in a Christian family. At age 19 he was fully captured for Christ and immediately consecrated himself to preach the gospel for the rest of his life. Early in his service, he met Watchman Nee, a renowned preacher, teacher, and writer. Witness Lee labored together with Watchman Nee under his direction. In 1934 Watchman Nee entrusted Witness Lee with the responsibility for his publication operation, called the Shanghai Gospel Bookroom.

Prior to the Communist takeover in 1949, Witness Lee was sent by Watchman Nee and his other co-workers to Taiwan to ensure that the things delivered to them by the Lord would not be lost. Watchman Nee instructed Witness Lee to continue the former's publishing operation abroad as the Taiwan Gospel Bookroom, which has been publicly recognized as the publisher of Watchman Nee's works outside China. Witness Lee's work in Taiwan manifested the Lord's abundant blessing. From a mere 350 believers, newly fled from the mainland, the churches in Taiwan grew to 20,000 in five years.

In 1962 Witness Lee felt led of the Lord to come to the United States, settling in California. During his 35 years of service in the U.S., he ministered in weekly meetings and weekend conferences, delivering several thousand spoken messages. Much of his speaking has since been published as over 400 titles. Many of these have been translated into over fourteen languages. He gave his last public conference in February 1997 at the age of 91.

He leaves behind a prolific presentation of the truth in the Bible. His major work, *Life-study of the Bible,* comprises over 25,000 pages of commentary on every book of the Bible from the perspective of the believers' enjoyment and experience of God's divine life in Christ through the Holy Spirit. Witness Lee was the chief editor of a new translation of the New Testament into Chinese called the Recovery Version and directed the translation of the same into English. The Recovery Version also appears in a number of other languages. He provided an extensive body of footnotes, outlines, and spiritual cross references. A radio broadcast of his messages can be heard on Christian radio stations in the United States. In 1965 Witness Lee founded Living Stream Ministry, a non-profit corporation, located in Anaheim, California, which officially presents his and Watchman Nee's ministry.

Witness Lee's ministry emphasizes the experience of Christ as life and the practical oneness of the believers as the Body of Christ. Stressing the importance of attending to both these matters, he led the churches under his care to grow in Christian life and function. He was unbending in his conviction that God's goal is not narrow sectarianism but the Body of Christ. In time, believers began to meet simply as the church in their localities in response to this conviction. In recent years a number of new churches have been raised up in Russia and in many eastern European countries.

OTHER BOOKS PUBLISHED BY
Living Stream Ministry

Titles by Witness Lee:

Abraham—Called by God	0-7363-0359-6
The Experience of Life	0-87083-417-7
The Knowledge of Life	0-87083-419-3
The Tree of Life	0-87083-300-6
The Economy of God	0-87083-415-0
The Divine Economy	0-87083-268-9
God's New Testament Economy	0-87083-199-2
The World Situation and God's Move	0-87083-092-9
Christ vs. Religion	0-87083-010-4
The All-inclusive Christ	0-87083-020-1
Gospel Outlines	0-87083-039-2
Character	0-87083-322-7
The Secret of Experiencing Christ	0-87083-227-1
The Life and Way for the Practice of the Church Life	0-87083-785-0
The Basic Revelation in the Holy Scriptures	0-87083-105-4
The Crucial Revelation of Life in the Scriptures	0-87083-372-3
The Spirit with Our Spirit	0-87083-798-2
Christ as the Reality	0-87083-047-3
The Central Line of the Divine Revelation	0-87083-960-8
The Full Knowledge of the Word of God	0-87083-289-1
Watchman Nee—A Seer of the Divine Revelation ...	0-87083-625-0

Titles by Watchman Nee:

How to Study the Bible	0-7363-0407-X
God's Overcomers	0-7363-0433-9
The New Covenant	0-7363-0088-0
The Spiritual Man 3 volumes	0-7363-0269-7
Authority and Submission	0-7363-0185-2
The Overcoming Life	1-57593-817-0
The Glorious Church	0-87083-745-1
The Prayer Ministry of the Church	0-87083-860-1
The Breaking of the Outer Man and the Release ...	1-57593-955-X
The Mystery of Christ	1-57593-954-1
The God of Abraham, Isaac, and Jacob	0-87083-932-2
The Song of Songs	0-87083-872-5
The Gospel of God 2 volumes	1-57593-953-3
The Normal Christian Church Life	0-87083-027-9
The Character of the Lord's Worker	1-57593-322-5
The Normal Christian Faith	0-87083-748-6
Watchman Nee's Testimony	0-87083-051-1

Available at
Christian bookstores, or contact Living Stream Ministry
2431 W. La Palma Ave. • Anaheim, CA 92801
1-800-549-5164   • www.livingstream.com